ALASKA'S
TOTEM
POLES

BY PAT KRAMER

FOREWORD BY DAVID A. BOXLEY

Alaska Northwes
Anchorage ● Po

D0166832

To all totem pole carvers whose names are lost in time.

I'd like to acknowledge all Totem People, especially Frank L. Fulmer, Tlingit carver; David R. Boxley and Wayne Hewson, Tsimshian artisans from Metlakatla; and the many Native people throughout Alaska and British Columbia who have invited me to countless ceremonies and kindly explained their stories, dances, and traditions so that they might be recorded with respect and honor. Thank you to Sealaska Heritage Institute and the Alaska Native Language Center, as well as Richard Dauenhauer for assisting with tribal name pronunciation guides, and to Donald Gregory for his helpful review.

Second printing 2005

Library of Congress Cataloging-in-Publication Data

Kramer, Pat.
  Alaska's totem poles / by Pat Kramer.
    p. cm.
Includes bibliographical references and index.
  ISBN 0-88240-585-3
  1. Totem poles—Alaska—History. 2. Indians of North America—Material culture—Alaska. 3. Indian wood-carving—Alaska—History. 4. Indians of North America—Alaska—Antiquities. 5. Alaska—Antiquities. I. Title.

E98.T65K73 2003
979.8004'9712 —dc22

                              2003021338

Photo Captions: *Cover*—This contemporary totem pole in Ketchikan depicts a carver holding his adz. *Title page*—Haines totem pole.

Archival Photo Credits: *Title page image* © Alaska Division of Community and Business Development; *Page 24*, Mrs. Forrest Hunt photo, MSCUA, University of Washington Libraries, negative number NA3610; *Page 34*, Clarence Leroy Andrews photo, MSCUA, University of Washington Libraries, negative number NA2890; *Page 39*, Otto C. Schallerer photo, MSCUA, University of Washington Libraries, negative number NA3854.

Alaska Northwest Books®
An imprint of Graphic Arts Center Publishing Company
P.O. Box 10306, Portland, Oregon 97296-0306
503-226-2402; www.gacpc.com

President: Charles M. Hopkins
Associate Publisher: Douglas A. Pfeiffer
Editorial Staff: Timothy W. Frew, Tricia Brown, Kathy Howard, Jean Andrews, Jean Bond-Slaughter
Editor: Ellen Harkins Wheat
Production Staff: Richard L. Owsiany, Susan Dupere
Design: Constance Bollen, cb graphics
Map: Gray Mouse Graphics

PRINTED IN THE UNITED STATES OF AMERICA

CONTENTS

YUKON
TERRITORY

ALASKA

1
Fairbanks

Anchorage
2

AREA OF
MAP

Juneau

Yakutat

CANADA
U.S.

Chilkat
River

Klukwan
3
Haines
Skagway

ALASKA

Taku
River

Juneau
4

**NATIVE
REGIONS**

Tlingit

Haida

Tsimshian

NORTH

PACIFIC

OCEAN

Hoonah
5

6
Angoon

7
Sitka

8 Kake

N

W

S

BRITISH
COLUMBI

9 Wrangell
(Fort Wrangell)

Prince of
Wales Island

Stikine River

**WHERE TO VIEW
ALASKA'S TOTEMS**

1. Alaskaland Pioneer
   Park
2. Alaska Native
   Heritage Center;
   Alaska Native
   Medical Center
3. Klukwan;
   Fort Seward (Haines);
   Sheldon Museum and
   Cultural Center
4. Alaska State Museum;
   City walking tours
5. Hoonah
6. Angoon
7. Sitka National Historic
   Park
8. Kake
9. Wrangell Museum;
   Chief Shakes Tribal
   House of the Bear;
   Kiks'Adi Totem Park
10. Klawock
11. Kasaan
12. Hydaburg
13. Totem Heritage Center;
    Totem Bight State Park
14. Saxman Totem Village
15. Metlakatla

Tuxekan
(abandoned)

Klawock
10 **11**

Old Kasaan
(abandoned)
Kasaan

Ketchikan
13
Saxman

Hydaburg
12

Sukkwan
(abandoned)
14

Howkan
(abandoned)
15 Metlakatla

Klinkwan
(abandoned)
Annette
Island

Dixon Entrance

Na
Riv

Queen
Charlotte
Islands
(Haida
Gwaii)

Masset

Port Simpson
(Fort Simpson)

Old Metlakatla

Prince Rupert

Skeena Riv

Foreword

Totem poles are the physical evidence, the touchable results of eons of Native history and tradition carried on in the songs and dances of our people. Even today in these modern times, they still matter.

Totem pole carvers, the artists who created these monuments, were the vessels by which the culture traveled. They had to be knowledgeable about oral history and carving styles. They were often called upon by distant villages and tribes to create works of art that would say to anyone who visited: this is who lives here. These are the stories, the history of this man, this clan, this village.

The arrival of non-Natives on theses shores brought many changes. The subsistence-based lifestyle was overrun by a wage-based existence, and the introduction of epidemic diseases and the influence of missionaries caused the disruption of the master/apprentice carver system. Native art, so close to and tied in with our cultural ceremonies, fell victim to the results of these extreme changes. Since the 1950s, though, the art has made a strong comeback. There are excellent carvers and culture bearers from all of the First Nations tribes leading and carrying on the art, language, and culture for the next generation.

Still, some things are hard to change . . . you would think that in these modern times, misconceptions and misinformation about Native people and totem poles would have been long ago "educated out" of non-Native people. Example: When I was a young boy I received a game for Christmas called "Fort Apache." It consisted of a number of plastic soldiers, Indians in various battle poses, a fort, teepees, cactus, and, *of course*, totem poles. Even though the Natives outside the Northwest Coast never had totem poles! Well, that was forty years ago, and it couldn't happen today . . . right? Recently I took some apprentices to Iowa to install a totem pole at a university in Dubuque. One of my companions, who knew of my Fort Apache story, purchased a plastic-wrapped toy for me in a gift shop there. It consisted of a cowboy, an Indian, and guess what? Yep, a totem pole.

So, I and others have been on this journey, as Native artists and culture bearers, hopefully to show that we as Northwest Native people are still here celebrating our culture, and creating these unique works of art. They are as important now as they were in the beginning.

As a carver, I spend weeks working on a cedar log to create a totem pole, whether it be for a Native or non-Native client. But each time that pole is raised, it is such an amazing, emotional experience. It makes me feel so connected. So fortunate to be a Native artist, having the opportunity to make a positive contribution.

Totem poles are so much more than carved cedar. They literally stand for who we are.

—David A. Boxley
Metlakatla, Alaska, and Kingston, Washington

1

An Introduction to Alaska's Totems

As travelers leave Seattle and Puget Sound and head north toward Alaska, they sail up the Inside Passage, through deeply etched channels, bays, and fjords of coastal British Columbia and the Alaska Panhandle, also known as Southeast Alaska. This navigable edge of North America is exceptionally beautiful, with snowcapped mountains, rain-soaked cedar forests, and majestic glaciers spilling into the sea. On the journey, as travelers scan the shoreline, clusters of aged totem poles suddenly appear, looming in the mist. Calling silently to the eagles and ravens diving overhead, their soaring presence seems to symbolize something deep and mysterious.

The Totem People

Totem poles and the rich traditions associated with them originated in North America among the Native peoples who made their home along this jagged coastline of the North Pacific. Totems, fascinating monuments carved from cedar, are unique human attempts initiated in a time long ago to create a

---

Ancient tales involving Raven as creator, trickster,
and transformation expert are often depicted on totem poles.

record of each generation's presence and passing.

From north to south, North America's Totem People are classified by the languages they speak. The Tlingit (KLIN-kit or TLIN-kit) and Eyak (EE-yack) speakers are the Northwest Coast Indians who have lived in Alaska from ancient times. Two more recent arrivals are the Haida (HIDE-uh) and the Tsimshian (SIM-she-an) peoples. These groups share many cultural practices, including the making of totem poles.

Sharing in Alaska's totem tradition are several tribes from the province of British Columbia, Canada, and northern Washington state, extending approximately 900 miles as the crow flies along the western

Tsimshian carver Wayne Hewson, wearing traditional garb, next to a Bear Mother totem in Metlakatla.

Pacific coastline. Together these Native tribes make up the Totem People.

Originally, totem poles with their intricately carved figures were meant to convey important messages to passersby about the family and social status of the people who lived in a particular house in a certain village. Carved from a huge red or yellow cedar log, a totem pole allowed related members of a family clan to portray their family rights and stories through displaying authorized crests, or symbolic figures. Oft-depicted crest figures in Alaska included Raven, Wolf, Eagle, Bear, Whale, Frog, as well as an assortment of heroes and mythical creatures. Tribal members could view a totem and, seeing the crests, could identify the following: the family's lineage, its clan rights and prerogatives, its significant accomplishments, and its prestige. A few crests told the story of the people's migration into their present homeland, often relayed as stories of Raven leading them on a great journey. Other crests explained the family link to the spirit world of nature; for example, members of the Blackfish (or Killer Whale) clan believed that one of their ancestors once visited the Orca underwater village and, before returning, received a magical seaweed blanket, copper canoe, and other crests now exclusive to them.

The formal granting of crests for use on totem poles and other artifacts was a solemn part of an important ceremony known as the potlatch. Once officially sanctioned, these crests became rallying points to which each family member pledged his/her allegiance. Totem crests were exchanged through generations of alliances, intermarriage, and the payments of indemnities for wrongs done. Despite early misunderstandings by missionaries and outsiders in general, totem poles were not worshipped.

Totem poles come in several forms, including greet figures, memorial or mortuary poles, heraldic poles, house front poles, and even ridicule or shame poles. Territorial totem markers—a totem crest cut into a live tree—were most notable among the Tlingit, but all used them. Greet figures were 10- to

ALASKA'S NORTHWEST COAST INDIAN TRIBES

From earliest known times, Tlingit people have resided along the Alaska Panhandle between Icy Bay in the north and the Dixon Entrance in the south. Sometime during the seventeenth century, a century or more before the Russians and Europeans began to arrive, a small group of Haida people, originally from the Queen Charlotte Islands (Haida Gwaii) in Canada, arrived on the southern half of Prince of Wales Island. Setting up their own villages, sometimes on the exact place of abandoned Tlingit sites, either though arrangement with the Tlingit or by warring conquest, they settled and became known as the Kaigani Haida. Eventually, Tlingit and Haida peoples interacted, intermarried, and influenced each other's cultural traditions including totem pole crests, stories, and styles of carving. Today Alaska's Haida number around 300 individuals. Their reputation for excellence in totem carving far outweighs their numbers.

As for Alaska's Tsimshian, in 1887 a group of 823 people whose totem traditions originated around the Nass and Skeena Rivers in British Columbia, Canada, emigrated to an officially designated reservation on Annette Island. Following the beliefs of Anglican-influenced Father William Duncan, this determined group established a "Victorian enclave in the wilderness," and left behind their totem-carving ways. This settlement's traditional totem practices lay dormant until the 1970s, when a renaissance began with the arrival of two culture bearers who taught songs and dances. Also, carver Jack Hudson returned to Metlakatla and began teaching. •

12-foot-high figures of a single creature such as Bear, or a human. A memorial totem raised after an elder's death displayed all the crests a deceased person had acquired during his or her lifetime. A mortuary pole displayed all these authorized crests and either housed a coffin at the top or contained a small niche for the deceased's ashes. The heraldic totem was similar to a complex family coat of arms. A house front pole could be placed inside or outside a house to tell the heroic stories of the owning family, and it often served as the doorway to a huge clan house. Ridicule poles were meant to humiliate one's enemies or simply poke fun at someone, and a few interesting examples still exist today. For example, Saxman Totem Village in Ketchikan has a ridicule pole that portrays William H. Seward, noted for his role in purchasing Alaska from the Russians. Though the locals treated him with respect and gave him gifts, he was unaware that reciprocal gift-giving was custom, and he appeared rude. The pole displays him with his ears and nose stained red, signifying stinginess.

The meanings of totem poles have evolved greatly since contact with Europeans in the late 1700s. One traditional Tlingit origin myth states that long ago, the Old Ones were inspired to carve totems after finding a fully

IT ALL BEGINS WITH RAVEN

Tlingit stories describe how the Old Ones, led by Raven, traveled from a far away land via the Taku or Stikine River corridors to the place of frozen glaciers. Under Raven's guidance, four brave Tlingit women swam through a dangerous ice passage enclosed within a magical glacier cavern. Returning, they led the rest of their people to the land they now inhabit in southeastern Alaska. Before contact, in Pacific Northwest Coast Native belief systems, the world owed its form to Raven, a supernatural creature whose character combined the attributes of spirit, transformer, fool, creator, human, bird, genius, and trickster. Ranging at least as far as the Koriak tribes of eastern Siberia, stories describe Raven as the original ravenous creature with a legendary curiosity. With his out-of-control appetites, Raven was considered the author of all nature's major phenomena—sun, moon, stars, wind, tides, animals, and cedar trees. In stories that are surprisingly similar, Raven's antics also accounted for the creation of humans and their arrival in specific regions on earth. Stories such as these provide tantalizing glimpses into Alaska Native history, hint at where the ancestors may have lived, and teach respect for the natural world. ●

This replicated Tlingit clan house, painted with the Raven crest, stands in Totem Bight State Historical Park, Ketchikan.

carved log washed up on a sandy beach. In another story, the Haida tell of a master carver who, after seeing the reflection of a totem-dotted village deep within the ocean, created a house front and several poles overnight, and then taught his fellow villagers how to carve. Originally, totems were strictly bound up with the kinship system of the people who made them. Today, totem crests are used to express Alaska's pride in all of its people, the land, its commemorative occasions, flourishing cultures, and rich traditions.

The Importance of Cedar

Totem poles evolved in a region of the world noted for annual precipitation levels ranging from 112 to 200 inches per year. From Southeast Alaska to the Copper River Delta, the temperate rain forests are renowned for their cathedral-like beauty. Western red cedar, the preferred wood for carving totem poles, is widespread in southern Alaska coastal regions, out-competes Alaska yellow cedar where their ranges overlap, and begins to thin out near Ketchikan and the southern end of Prince of Wales Island. From this area north, Alaska yellow cedar, often preferred by northern totem carvers, is the dominant species growing in the Southeast's boggy and rocky areas. Since Alaska's northern forests lack red cedar, the locals developed an active trading system with southern tribes to acquire any giant red cedar logs they desired.

Western red cedar can range in color from reddish cinnamon to rich sienna brown and has a soft, satin luster, while the wood of Alaska yellow cedar ranges from mellow amber to golden yellow. The oil in cedar makes it resistant to decay and insect infestation. Growing up to 200 feet tall, well-established red cedar trees can live for about 1,000 years, while yellow cedar trees commonly range from 1,000 to 1,500 years in age. Growing in mixed forests with other conifer species such as Douglas fir, western hemlock, Pacific yew, and Sitka spruce, cedar surpasses them all for its workability. Distinguished by its straight grain, ease of splitting, uniform texture, and the absence of pitch, cedar carves as easily as cold butter and yet holds a fine edge.

Cedar's unique physical properties have influenced both the practical and spiritual life of Northwest Coast Indians. The tree, a gift from Raven and often respectfully referred to as an esteemed "sister," was used to construct house planks and pillars for traditional post-and-beam community lodges or clan houses. Within each clan house, six or seven sets of related parents,

---

Tomas de Suria, shipboard artist with the Malaspina expeditions of 1793, recorded this view of a Grizzly Mortuary Pole at Yakutat.

Women wove and painted cedar items including waterproof hats, as in this photograph by Edward S. Curtis, ca. 1915.

grandparents, and children—perhaps 30 to 50 people—lived their lives. Woodworkers also utilized cedar to make hundreds of utilitarian and ceremonial objects including ornately carved interior house posts, masks for elaborate ceremonial dances, rattles, and drum logs, steambent fishhooks, spears, and fish clubs, bentwood boxes for storage, and household food containers, cradles and mortuary boxes as well as totem poles. Girls learned from their grandmothers how to skillfully shred red cedar bark strips, roll them into ropes and fish nets, or weave them into waterproof hats, capes, and skirts. Yellow cedar required soaking and boiling before it was pounded into strips, interwoven with duck down or mountain goat wool, and made into soft blankets. Women also made coiled cedar-root baskets decorated with geometric patterns formed from grass stems and black tree bark. Skilled artisans ornamented all of these items with family crests.

Some believe that in ancient times, Northwest Coastal peoples made totem carvings that were smaller in scale. Old totem poles the size of a walking cane are on display in some museum collections. As Alaska's Native peoples acquired metal tools through contact with explorers, the ease and speed of carving increased, and Indian houses and totem poles increased in size and number. Before contact, master carvers made coloring agents from ground-up stones and salmon eggs mixed with sea water and saliva, creating hues more accurately described as stains. After contact, the use of commercially produced house paint swiftly came into use.

Individuals used cottonwood dugout canoes for fishing in tidepools or moving about. But groups of warriors or hunters on long commutes paddled large oceangoing dugout red cedar canoes, seating up to 50 people. To make these huge canoes, skilled artisans, using chisels made from yew wood, antler, and stone, cut a notch into the trunk of a huge growing tree. Setting a small controlled fire, they burned the notch wider, opening the gap until the tree toppled over. Workers then split the trunk open and chopped out a channel. Filling the channel with water and hot stones that caused it to boil, they steamed out the heartwood and pried open the remaining shell. The paddlers' cross-braced seats served to keep the boat taut. The Haida manufactured transport canoes legendary for their size and speed, and the Tlingit sometimes bartered with them for fully completed vessels.

In return, the Haida prized the huge yellow cedar logs found in Tlingit territory. This variety was especially desired for digging sticks, bows, masks, dishes, paddles, and particularly distinguished totem poles. Able navigators swarmed the ocean while Native traders guarded overland trade routes up over the Coast Range to Indian tribes of the Interior. Authorized persons were responsible for transporting boxes filled with fatty fish paste, alternately known as eulachon or candlefish grease, plus furs, dried salmon, carved masks, shells, and other desirable coastal items. The trade routes were known as "grease trails."

Carving a Totem Pole

Cedar logs, once painstakingly felled by chisels and fire, today are swiftly brought down with chain saws. Cedar trees suitable for totem poles are found in the densest part of the forest. Here, trees compete for sunlight, branches grow solely on the upper third of the tree, and the trunks are tall and straight with few knots.

Once a felled tree trunk is safely placed inside the carving shed, the head carver assembles a team of one to five apprentices to help with the carving and

NO WORD FOR ART

Though the Totem People had no formal word for "art," they embellished their lives with carved and painted symbols, even applying crests onto every household item including spoons, bowls, and individual items of clothing. It was taken for granted that life was an unbroken tradition of creative expression filled with pictorial wisdom. ●

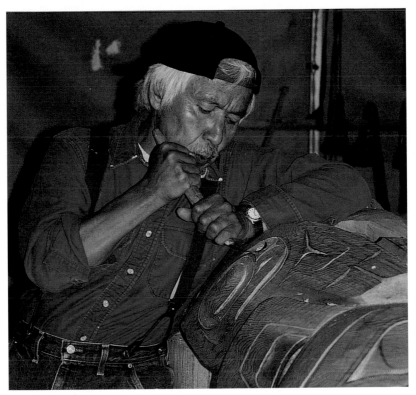

**Tlingit master carver Nathan Jackson puts finishing details on a totem
at Saxman Totem Park near Ketchikan.**

holds meetings with the people who have commissioned the pole. Knowledge
of exactly how to work totem crests is something that an apprentice carver learns
from years at a master carver's side. Those who are diligent helpers may someday
see their own names associated with carved masks and totems. After the totem's
patrons have indicated which crests they prefer, the master carver either adapts
old crest stories for them or creates new crests using traditional guidelines. To
understand a totem's meaning, it is necessary both to know what the patron
wanted and how the carver interpreted those requests. In ancient times, totem
pole stories and symbols were shared orally through the generations. Sometimes
stories were altered or lost. So in the case of a few very old totems, it is not
possible to fully interpret their meaning.

The average progress for a solo carver is about one foot per week. When several carvers participate, the work speeds up. The design of the totem pole is roughly drawn on a planning sheet, then it is transferred to the log itself. Modern carvers use power tools to rough out the shapes along the length of the enormous log. Traditional carvers once used adzes made from antler and hard yew wood, and carving tools with sharp blades made from obsidian glass obtained from volcanic cinder cones in the region.

On many old cedars, the center of the trunk is rotting away. To make the final pole lighter, easier to handle, and to prevent the pole from cracking as it dries, some carvers hollow out the back into a U-shape. Others leave the trunk intact. As the bark is removed, the heady fragrance of cedar oil fills the shed. Red cedar has an incenselike fragrance while yellow cedar smells like raw potatoes. Some carvers ask for an initial blessing ceremony to celebrate the emergence of the heartwood.

Throughout the carving process, the totem's patrons are expected to keep the carvers warm and happy. Besides feeding them and providing occasional entertainment, small gifts are given—from a gesture as simple as a few apples or a homemade pie to something as elaborate as a potluck dinner. The head carver is responsible for supervising the apprentices, who are usually given tasks on the upper end of the totem where mistakes are less visible.

Finally the day for the pole-raising ceremony draws near. The master carver meets with the elders of the tribe to create an approved agenda for the ceremonial raising procedures. The team moves the completed totem pole into position for the big day. The night before the raising, the patrons and the carvers host a private gala.

At the climactic raising event, elders in full regalia arrive in a procession, and the master carver is honored. Various members of the tribe perform dances, sing songs, make speeches, and give blessings. In the old days, crews of workers rolled the totem into an inclined trench about 20 feet in length. Gradually filling in the trench, they maneuvered ropes and pikes to coax the totem skyward. Today, it's usually a heavy machinery operator who makes quick work of raising a heavy totem pole. At the end of the ceremony, then as now, the patrons thank everyone in attendance with a small gift, ranging from an art print to a piece of fruit given in appreciation for the participants bearing witness to and thus validating the event. A community dinner—the requisite feasting—completes the day.

When a new Eagle totem honoring all Northwest Coast Indian tribes was raised in Vancouver, B.C., in 2000, invited guests came from as far away as Alaska and Seattle.

Owning a totem is expensive. Costs today vary from $100 to $5,000 per foot, depending on the reputation of the carver. Traditionally, master totem carvers invoke respect, and today some are internationally recognized. A few are beloved, as much for their willingness to teach their craft as for their extraordinary design and carving skills. Totem poles represent a cultural renaissance among Indian groups who only a century ago were reputed to be a dying people. Today's master carvers work diligently to keep totem traditions alive, and to pass them on to each new generation of carvers as vibrant testimony to their flourishing culture and its revival.

Early Totem Sightings

Though archaeologists claim that Pacific Northwest Coast Indians have occupied this region for about 10,000 years, Native historians like to say that the land was granted to the Old Ones from the beginning of time.

Since oral stories vary greatly, our totem detective story starts out less poetically with a survey of the journals of the first Russian, European, and American seagoing expeditions to Alaska's shores. Numerous documents indicate that when these early explorers arrived in the mid- to late-1700s, totem poles were an uncommon sight. While the Alaska Indian tradition of carving crests into a variety of stone, bone, shell, and wooden objects from spoons to grave markers has roots that go back for thousands of years, it was the post-contact spread of metal tools that encouraged a flurry of major building projects, including increased construction of large clan houses and ever more ornate totem poles.

Since there was no non-Native word for "totem pole" and outsiders were unfamiliar with Native traditions, ship's log keepers devised various words for their observations of carved monuments. In the decade after 1785, expedition records document the progression from few indications of these carvings to an American captain and his crew who helped to raise a totem pole.

Of France's La Pérouse party at Lituya Bay in 1786, the Tlingit were said to have responded to the strange sight of ships in this manner: "They seemed to be great black birds with immense white wings. . . . " The onboard ship's artist left engravings of the Tlingit people and their villages *without* totems. Visiting the Yakutat Tlingit in 1787, British Capt. George Dixon described the crests he saw on everyday objects as "figures . . . of hieroglyphics: fishes and other animals, heads of men and various whimsical designs." And British Capt. John Meares among the Haida in 1788 described both painted house fronts and "great wooden images."

Later the same year, the Nootka people of British Columbia's Vancouver Island spared the life of John R. Jewitt, the blacksmith aboard the American

THE FIRST DRAWINGS OF TOTEM POLES

John Webber, official artist for Capt. James Cook's third expedition in 1778, engraved a depiction of two Nootka house posts that he observed on what is now Canada's Vancouver Island. Due to the simplistic nature of this rendering and because only guests of high status were invited inside Native homes, some historians guess that Webber may have acted solely on verbal accounts of "posts decorated with faces," and may never have seen one firsthand. Not until 1791 did an eyewitness—seaman John Bartlett—sketch the first crude, but apparently accurate, ink image while traveling aboard the American trader *Gustavus*. Having viewed a scene at Dadens, a Haida village in what is now the Queen Charlotte Islands (Haida Gwaii), Bartlett made his drawing, and noted "the entrance was cut out of a large tree and carved all the way up and down." ●

trading vessel *Boston*, but forced him into slavery. After three years, he escaped and later wrote of "large trees carved and painted" where he had been captive. In 1791, French merchant Capt. Etienne Marchand described a Haida entrance door totem: "The head of this statue is dressed with a cap in the form of a sugar loaf..." adding pertinent information that the carvings were "of vibrant red, black and apple green color." And Spanish expedition Capt. Alejandro Malaspina supervised ship's artist José Cardero in his sketches of carved posts at Yakutat.

A year later, British Capt. George Vancouver described a double mortuary column, house poles, and detached totems. Then on a later expedition in 1793, Malaspina and his artist Tomás de Suria visiting the Tlingit at Lituya Bay recorded an upright Grizzly figure holding a mortuary box (see page 12). "We do not know whether the colossal monster . . . is an idol or merely a frightful record of the destructive nature of death. . . . The height of the monster was no less than ten and half feet."

It was in 1794 that Yankee trader Capt. H. Roberts, aboard the *Jefferson*, stopped at a Haida village on what would later be known as Dall Island, and became the first outsider to record the raising of a totem pole. "To ingratiate themselves . . . the captain with the carpenter and some of the crew went to the village to plane and smooth a wooden pole. The next day they returned with two spare top masts and the necessary tackle to raise the pole and set it in position." At the request of Chief Cunneah, Roberts' crew painted the pole, placed a carved "toad" on top, and raised it. There is no word on the celebrations that no doubt followed.

A review of these early expedition logs indicates that while monumental wooden carvings were not yet the overwhelming sights they would later become, they were present in small numbers. By 1799 and later, totem poles were more common. British seafarer Capt. George Dixon aboard the *Eliza* reported Haida communal mortuary poles at Kiusta. Two journal keepers, young John Boit aboard American Capt. Gray's *Columbia* and Robert Haswell, aboard the *Lady Washington*, both reported house entrance poles at Clayquot. Later, Louis Choris, lithographer with Russian explorer Otto von Kotzebue's voyage between 1815 and 1817, left many rich pictorial records of crest figures, though any representations he did of totem poles have been lost.

Beginning in 1784 and working their way eastward, Russian traders acting under the auspices of the Shelikov-Golikov Company began an accelerated

In 1791, seaman John Bartlett sketched this Haida house front pole and noted, "The passage into the house was between the teeth."

harvesting of sea otters. Quickly decimating the Aleutians, then the Kodiak region, the Southeast was their third and final stop. By the end of 1799, Tsar Paul I, son of the late Russian Empress Catherine the Great, granted sole trading rights to a new entity, the Russian-American Company, to handle territorial fur trade. Company manager and first governor of Russian Alaska, Alexander Baranov established forty posts, among them Fort St. Michael near present-day Sitka. Staffed with Russian convict labor and enslaved Tlingit and Aleut people, the frenetic harvesting operation of sea otter furs continued.

In June 1802, enraged Tlingit destroyed the fort, killing many and forcing Baranov to pay 10,000 rubles ransom for the survivors. Two years later, Baranov rebuilt a new settlement, naming it New Archangel and declaring it the capital of Russian America. It would later be renamed Sitka. In 1804, Baranov, aided with cannon fire from Russian Capt.-Lt. Urey Lisianski's ship *Neva*, retaliated against the Tlingit and many lives were lost. Of the mortuary boxes he observed after this battle, Lisianski wrote, "The bodies here are burned, and the ashes, together with the bones that remain unconsumed, deposited in wooden boxes which are placed on pillars that have different figures painted and carved on them, according to the wealth of the deceased. On taking possession of our new settlement we destroyed a hundred at least of these, and I examined many of the boxes . . . the colors were black, light green and dark red." Of monumental wooden carvings he wrote, "These families, however, always live apart; and, to distinguish the caste to which they belong, they place on the top of their houses, carved in wood or painted, the bird or beast that represents it."

The Golden Age of Totem Poles

Almost as soon as Russia dominated Alaska's fur trade, America's "Boston Men" and Britain's Hudson's Bay Company traders stubbornly made inroads into their monopoly. Sensing a profit to be made, in 1834 nine Tsimshian villages set up trading outposts just south of Alaska, outside Fort Simpson in British Columbia. Older village leaders appointed younger relatives to manage the new outposts. This turn of events resulted in a series of rivalry potlatches. Dozens of new totems were carved to sort out the newly elevated status of the outpost leaders.

Throughout Southeast Alaska, as Natives moved closer to communities where work was available, common people became richer than the elders they left behind. Whereas traditionally, only a few people could afford to commission a totem, from 1830 to 1880 hundreds of newly rich working people returned home to indulge in one of these big-ticket items. Historic photographs of coastal Alaska villages during the late 1880s and 1890s, sometimes called totems' Golden Age, show "forests of totem poles." But as epidemics ravaged the population over and over again, leadership crumbled, survivors became demoralized, and the unique and complex family system that included totem crests began to break down. Without slave labor, the upper and middle classes who occupied traditional longhouses found that no one was willing to cut and carry wood. Villagers moved into American-style bungalows on the outskirts of growing towns. The old villages, recently revitalized with new totem poles and clan houses, began to empty. Soon the rain forest encroached on doorways, weather eroded abandoned longhouses, and vines grew around untended totem poles.

By about 1860, for various reasons including the near extinction of sea otters, Russian interest in its Alaska territory declined. In 1867, U.S. Secretary of State William Seward negotiated the purchase of Alaska from Russia for

$7.2 million. Critics attacked the purchase as "Seward's Folly." The *New York Tribune* coined the term "Walrussia" for what was represented as a worthless, frozen wasteland. Historic as the transaction is portrayed, Native claims were not considered in the process. It took until 1924 for Congress to extend official citizenship to Native Americans.

Devastating Changes

The inroads that Christianity made among Native Alaskans was accelerated by the more than a century of periodic epidemics. As early as 1791, French surgeon Claude Roblet with the Marchand expedition, like Capt. Dixon before him, recorded signs of smallpox around the Sitka area. Throughout the 1800s, there may have been as many as six major epidemics of various diseases, some occurring simultaneously, others occurring a few decades apart. But the final blow to the old ways began in 1900 with the arrival of the "Great Death." Reeling from the effects of smallpox, measles, diphtheria, and pneumonia, Alaska's Indians experienced waves of polio and tuberculosis. Famine accompanied the deadly march of disease. In a period of 20 years, up to two-thirds of Alaska's Natives lost their lives.

Throughout these devastating periods, American missionaries tended to the sick and built orphanages. As a routine part of their ministering duties, Christian workers discouraged traditional practices as they sincerely tried to improve the Natives' lives. It was but a few religious leaders who were forward-thinking as well as charitable. For example, in 1882 Presbyterian missionaries John G. Brady (later territorial governor of Alaska) and Fannie Kellogg opened an old Sitka military barracks as a Tlingit training school. Though the original building burned to the ground, Rev. Sheldon Jackson organized a nationwide fund-raising campaign, and Sheldon Jackson College had its beginning in 1878. Shortly afterward, the Tlingit asked Jackson to establish a Tlingit mission near Haines.

As Presbyterian superintendent of the Home Missions of the Territories and later as First General Agent of Education in Alaska, Jackson worried that Native cultures would disappear. To this end, throughout his journeys he collected thousands of items including totem poles and placed them in educational displays. To house his collections in Sitka, construction began in 1895 on a museum that has been in use since 1897. One of Jackson's goals in establishing the museum was to help future generations of Alaska Natives learn

A COLLECTING FRENZY

During the 1800s, dozens of research voyages to Alaska were funded by various nations. "Science" was the buzzword of the day and scientific expeditions were very popular with the public. One example was an expedition supported by Russia's Academy of Sciences in 1839, in which scientist I. G. Voznesenskii was sent to study the region's Native populations. After a 10-year visit he brought back more than one thousand artifacts. Over the next century, travelers from sailors to religious clerics collected masks and carvings, helmets and clubs, rattles and fishhooks, bowls and boxes, blankets and combs. For a period of 40 years before and after the turn of the twentieth century, academics raced each other to build collections. Museum displays popularized three concepts: wild plants, wild animals, and "primitive" people.

Among the prominent researchers of the day, Captain J. A. Jacobsen boasted that he had personally acquired 7,000 Tlingit objects during a single expedition. Wealthy patrons collected artifacts, spurred on by the myth of a vanishing race. For example, J. L. Kraft, founder of Kraft Foods, collected Northwest Coast totem poles, one of which was long displayed on Chicago's lakefront.

As a result of this activity, early Alaskan Indian art pieces are displayed in legendary museums throughout the world ranging from the Museum of Fine Arts in St. Petersburg, Russia, to the Menil Collection in Houston, Texas.

Since 1990, with the implementation of the Native American Graves Protection and Repatriation Act (NAGPRA), Indian tribes have begun to exercise newly defined rights to Native American human remains, funerary objects, sacred objects, and cultural objects. The Act requires federal agencies and museums to provide information about Native American cultural items to parties with standing, and upon presentation of a valid request, dispose of or repatriate these objects to them. Subsequently many tribes throughout North America are either in active negotiation or prolonged court procedures to reclaim many of their former items. Several museums and collectors have responded. Notable among these were the takings from the 1899 Harriman Expedition. In July 2001, Seattle's Burke Museum along with the Peabody Essex Museum, the Field Museum, the National Museum of the American Indian, and Cornell University's Johnson Museum of Art repatriated house posts, a totem pole, and hundreds of cultural objects to descendants of the Cape Fox Tlingit tribe near Ketchikan. And in 2003, the Tlingit people in Angoon repatriated a Bear totem, the symbol of their *Teikweidi* or Bear clan. Disappearing about 1908, it had been located in six different locations on the Greeley campus of the University of Northern Colorado, where it inspired their sports team mascot, Totem Teddy. ●

In the Golden Age of Totem Poles, villages such as Howkan were studded with totems.

how their forebears lived. Today, both ongoing vocational programs and a collection at Sitka bear his name.

Most government educators and Christian missionaries, however, believed that totem poles were part of the old ways that needed to be enthusiastically discouraged. They demanded that Natives cease their carving and burn their poles. Totem-making virtually ceased by 1901, and the practices that went with the tradition slowly began to fade away.

Symbol of the Pacific Northwest

Set against this recurring devastation, and adapting to a glut of fur traders, government agents, and missionaries, by 1885, Alaska's Natives began to encounter a new group of outsiders. Pampered travelers began arriving from Seattle by steamship. These early tourists explored "the Last Frontier," marveled at Alaska's glaciers, and traveled ashore to purchase curios. Native artists shrewdly took the opportunity to produce souvenir totems. Next, prospectors and storekeepers began to arrive by the thousands. And scientific exploration also continued apace. Financed by railroad magnate Edward H. Harriman in 1899, a distinguished group of 126 famous and influential scientists, naturalists, artists, and writers assembled a "floating university" to study the new land. In the spirit of the times, they collected thousands of items including a few totem poles. Official photographers for the Harriman Expedition included the famed Edward S. Curtis, who took striking photos of villages complete with toppling poles. These pictures proved especially popular with the news media of the day, adding to the popularity of this unique Indian art form—totem poles.

In addition to academics and tourists, several well-attended international expositions made the concept of "totem poles" a household term. The 1876 Centennial Exposition in Philadelphia and the 1893 World's Columbia Exposition in Chicago both displayed a few traditional totem poles from Alaska along with a mixed assortment of other artifacts from Native peoples. A guidebook stated, "It is more than probable that the World's Columbia Exposition will furnish the last opportunity for an acquaintance with the 'noble red-man' before he achieves annihilation." For even as totems were rotting away in Alaska's Native villages, crowds of faraway strangers were identifying the totem pole as the new symbol of the Pacific Northwest Coast. However it wasn't until the government organized large-scale restoration efforts in the 1930s, and dedicated enthusiasts researched and revived the old ways in the 1960s and 1970s, that Pacific Northwest Coast totem art and its related ceremonies experienced a full and rich renaissance. ■

2

Totem Traditions

The meanings and traditions surrounding totem poles have steadily evolved over the past two centuries. While ancient totems were a series of authorized crests and story figures indicating the totem owner's family position within their household, and ultimately within their tribe, they also spoke of clan history, of debts and repayments. Today the focus of totem poles is greater. Skillful Native master carvers improvise new crests based on traditional forms to immortalize their village founders, celebrate an historic state occasion, a scientific discovery, or cooperation between groups.

Pacific Northwest Coast Indian Society

To understand the traditional meaning of totems, ethnographers have spent more than 150 years sorting out how indigenous Alaskans once organized their social structure and kinship systems. At the time of contact, the Tlingit, Eyak, Haida, and Tsimshian peoples divided their households into three levels: an upper ruling class, a middle level of commoners, and slaves.

A museum diorama depicts a Tlingit chief wearing a Chilkat blanket and a woven cedar neck piece, a symbol of his authority.

Highest in rank were the chiefs, subchiefs, and elders responsible for the bureaucratic leadership of their households and villages. They administrated day-to-day living, marriages, adoptions, potlatches, inheritance rights, hunting expeditions, and building projects. To avenge wrongs, they initiated and led war parties, kidnapped slaves, plundered booty, and had transgressors punished. At dance gatherings and potlatches, they wore distinctive ceremonial dress, performed special dances, told exclusive stories, raised totem poles, bestowed thousands of gifts, and displayed shield-shaped objects called "coppers," a symbol of wealth. Some shared healing duties with the shaman. Elders at this level enjoyed privacy screens in their section of the communal house, the warmest place by the fire, first choice of fresh game, and the finest crafted objects. They had rights to the best fishing places on the river and the most productive hunting areas in the forest. Furthermore, their relatives monopolized the best trade routes and their women held exclusive picking rights to the best berry patches.

Next in line was a class of commoners that included artisans, traders, and other ordinary folks. Always hoping to be elevated to the upper ranks through marriage or adoption, the men ingratiated themselves to the upper classes through performing specialized tasks for which they were paid. This included activities ranging from serving as members of hunting parties, the manufacture of hunting or fishing implements and bentwood boxes, to the carving of masks and totem poles.

Women passed on their family names to their children and enjoyed the rights associated with the husband they married. Upper-class women, called "princesses" in stories, led a life of relative leisure, whereas middle-class women could expect to earn goods primarily from creating ceremonial costume pieces; spinning, dying, and weaving blankets; or making waterproof cedar-bark clothing. Rightfully belonging, at least in name, to the Chilkat people of the village of Klukwan, the knowledge to design and weave crest-laden Chilkat blankets also spread among many tribes. Except for ceremonial occasions, there were no set mealtimes. Long strips of dried salmon and game, a kind of "jerky," hung from the rafters of the house, and family members helped themselves. At low tide, people walked out to the oyster and clam beds. Slave women were expected to keep supplies of dried berry rolls, boiled salmon, deer, or cooked seal meat handy in a place near the fire.

**Tsimshian warriors wear traditional slatted wooden armor in reenactments
of plundering raids or in defending their villages.**

At the bottom of the social scale were slaves captured in war raids or born
to other slaves. Treated as property with no personal freedom, they performed
menial work like latrine duty, serving others, and keeping the fires lit. Slaves
were traded or freed as their owners wished. For elite families, slaves provided
them with an important source of free labor for producing surplus goods both
for trade and gift-giving.

To show one's rank and identity within this class system, people embellished their personal objects with a selection of crests owned communally
through their family lineage. Authorized symbols were present on house fronts,
interior and exterior walls, war canoes, weapons, storage boxes, eating utensils,
ceremonial masks and costumes, apparel, personal blankets, shirts, footwear,

jewelry, and of course, totem poles. Some Haida even tattooed their clan crests on their arms, legs, chests, and backs. Displaying a new crest on household items meant that a family member had advanced in social position.

Besides a relationship to one's mother, father, uncles, aunts, cousins, and so on, each person was classified within a kinship system comparable to a corporate management structure. The largest family divisions, called moieties or phratries, were first subdivided into clans or local lineages, then subdivided again into smaller units called houses. Each division was identified with a series of authorized crests, rights, wonders, and privileges. "Owning" crests meant that a moiety, clan, or house had sole rights to display authorized emblems. And those emblems signaled specific rights—such as owning the best fishing areas—exercised exclusively by them. "Wonders" were claims to favors from supernatural spirits, and "privileges" were daily benefits such as being served first, second, or third in what we might today call protocol.

TALKING STICKS

Prominent on two totems flanking the clan house at Totem Bight State Historical Park, "talking sticks" or "speaker's staffs" once indicated who was responsible for making policy within a household. About the size of a tall wood walking stick, and emblazoned with carved household crests, this implement entitled anyone who held it to make speeches and propose rules. Listeners who fell asleep during the proceedings sometimes awoke with a start to find the staff thrust into their hands. It was considered wise to mutter something about how great the speechmaker was. Some historians believe that these sticks were the precursors to totem poles. ●

An elder holds a talking stick,
a policy-making symbol.

Southeast Alaska's Native kinship system was matrilineal. Each person's name and status were passed down at birth from one's mother. And while tribal grandmothers played a special role in ceremonial occasions, rules for the household and all-important privileges, rights, and prerogatives were passed down from one's male relatives—specifically one's father and uncles.

Children's names and entitlements were tracked from birth, and individuals were always on the lookout for ways to boost their hereditary standing by rendering indispensable or possibly heroic services. Since a person's lineage was so influential, disagreements arose, and it was a punishable offense to use another's names, rights, or crests. Fortunate indeed were those who earned additional rights through formal adoption into a new clan, lineage, or house.

Older family members arranged marriages, but the complications of choosing a spouse were many. The Tlingit classified their upper two moieties either as Raven and Eagle, or Raven and Wolf, while the Haida assigned their upper moieties as Raven and Eagle. The Tsimshian identified four topmost divisions: Raven, Eagle, Wolf, and Killer Whale. When choosing a marriage partner, choices were limited to persons from the opposite moiety followed by several other taboos and restrictions. For example, an Eagle could only marry a Raven, and vice versa, giving rise to the concept of the Eagle and the Raven being known in totem lore as "lovebirds." Even among the Tsimshian, there were only two marriage groups: the Raven and Killer Whale clans chose from the Wolf and Eagle clans, and vice versa. Elders were brought in to resolve who-was-allowed-to-marry-whom conflicts. Sometimes, if elders liked a couple, they found loopholes. Marriage was a serious commitment, though a form of divorce was common. During his lifetime, a man averaged three wives, while titled widows received a designated living allowance and were the responsibility of their husband's brothers.

The Traditional Potlatch

Within this complex social system, keeping track of one's status and legal rights was a must. And the potlatch ceremony was the official means to validate rights and status. Lasting for up to three weeks, the potlatch celebration distributed bounty, formalized shifting loyalties, and legalized an individual's claims to names, crests, and privileges.

In this Tlingit pole at Totem Bight, a stately Eagle, sometimes called Thunderbird, stands over Killer Whale, also known as Blackfish.

Starting with several days of speeches and the parading of crests, through the long redressing of transgressions and crimes followed by the granting of new privileges, potlatch ceremonies culminated with feasting and sharing of gifts. For the climax, usually a totem pole was raised to formalize the granting of new crests, followed by solemn late-night secret ceremonies and masked dances.

A COMPLEX SOCIETY BASED ON SALMON RUNS

Freshly caught salmon are smoked over a pungent alderwood fire in the traditional manner.

Among the world's original societies, complicated social class divisions and kinship systems usually developed among agricultural people, such as the ancient Egyptians, rather than among hunter-gatherers. So early academics were surprised when they encountered a multilevel class and rights system well instituted among the first peoples of the Pacific Northwest and Alaska. Scholars believe that it was the assured annual gathering of thousands of salmon, the ever-abundant tidal pools, the proliferation of berry patches, and therefore the assured food supply, that acted like a regular agricultural harvest. There is a Tlingit saying, "When the tide is out, the table is set." Once a food supply is assured, people have the leisure time to develop and establish complicated social and ceremonial systems. The Indians of the Northwest Coast also benefited from a relatively moderate climate, making their life free from extreme hardship. ●

Traditionally, the Tlingit hosted a potlatch for elite funerals, piercing noble children's ears, or when a new heir replaced the mother's brother. Today the Tlingit are noted for potlatch ceremonies known as "Haa." One type of Haa honors a deceased relative in a crying ceremony—the last time to formally weep for the departed. To soothe the grieving, guests display art pieces once owned by the deceased. Other types of Haa resolutely reaffirm Tlingit cultural traditions, heal the spirit, or plead for peace through a designated holy woman. The Haida people traditionally held a potlatch to

POTLATCH WITNESSES

Tlingit men and boys from Hoonah dressed in ceremonial clothing to pose around a miniature cannon in this 1912 photo.

During the potlatch ceremony, certain persons were selected to receive a boost in social status. Designated witnesses were instructed to attentively watch the proceedings while the person received his or her new honors. After the induction ceremony, the witnesses were rewarded for their rapt attention with one or more gifts. If the honored person's new rights were ever questioned, the witnesses were expected to come at their own expense and give testimony as to what they had seen during the potlatch. Without written records, "witnessing" was the accepted way to keep track of significant events. ●

celebrate each house leader's investiture and again to memorialize his death, while today's Haida celebrate potlatches for specific people and their lifelong contributions to the community. The Tsimshian once held potlatches to mark the death of a leader. Their traditional and impressive potlatches today, characterized by a colorful leader who regulates the drummers, are held to reinstate a person's traditional family lineage and reaffirm their strong heritage.

Gift-giving is a major feature of the potlatch. Before contact, potlatch gifts might include rattles, furs, jewelry, robes, headpieces, bentwood boxes, and hand-woven blankets for the upper class, with berries and fish grease for ordinary folks. After contact, gifts modernized to sewing machines, wash basins, baby clothes, hard tack, flour, sugar, traps, guns, canoes, crockery, dishes, beds, mattresses, and the ever-popular blankets. Anyone who accepted a gift was expected to bear witness to the honors being granted and to support changes in the social fabric. Afterward, the highest-ranking guests were obliged to invite everyone to reciprocal potlatches where they presented better gifts.

The potlatch was never outlawed in Alaska, though for many years American government and church officials discouraged all Native cultural practices. If our modern American system kept track of legalities through a system similar to the potlatch, and if the potlatching were then outlawed, as it was in Canada in 1884, the following institutions would be discontinued. There would be no record of land or property ownership, old age or widow's pensions, insurance payouts, health benefits, court proceedings, criminal transgressors or punishments, hunting and fishing licenses, honors or medals bestowed, military service, births, marriages, and deaths. The ensuing chaos would be hard to fathom, though this is similar to what happened to Alaska's Natives when the potlatch was discouraged. Because of its central role legally, culturally, politically, economically, spiritually, and ceremonially, the potlatch was the fundamental means of transmitting and enforcing laws, status, order, good government, and wisdom.

When totem pole carving and the giving of traditional potlatches simultaneously ceased in Alaska around 1900 and the last great traditional Tlingit potlatch was held in 1904, a long barren period took hold in which Southeast Alaska's traditional Indian ceremonial practices nearly ceased.

Harvesting Decayed Totems

During the first third of the twentieth century, totem carving was generally defunct in Alaska. Fortunately, a few far-seeing individuals carried out sporadic efforts to preserve the poles that remained. Alaska's District Governor John G. Brady assembled a sizable collection of Tlingit and Haida totems, first displaying them at the 1903 Louisiana Purchase Exposition, then transporting them to the famous 1904 St. Louis World's Fair, and later to Portland's 1905 Lewis and Clark Exposition. The Alaska displays at these fairs, with their lofty totem poles and carved house fronts, attracted enthusiastic crowds. The well-traveled totems were eventually repatriated to Sitka, first reserved as a public park by President Harrison in 1890, and then established as Sitka National Monument in 1910. These totems stand today at Old Sitka, the location where the Kiks.ádi Tlingit people, barricaded in a log-stockade fort called Sish-kee-nu, resisted a Russian attack in October 1804.

Remarkably, not a single totem was to be found at Seattle's energetic 1909 Alaska-Yukon-Pacific Exposition. In 1913, clans from the Tlingit village of Kake destroyed all their totem poles. Twenty-four historical photographs of

Old totems lie where they fall until clan descendants pay to have them duplicated. Decay-resistant cedar will start to deteriorate after about 60 years.

that village taken about the year 1900 were all that remained, and they lay forgotten in a library archive. Today, those photographs are on display at the Kake Tribal Corporation Offices, though it took almost 70 years for the photos to inspire the building of new totems, including the world's tallest totem.

By Presidential Proclamation in 1916, Old Kasaan, a Haida enclave on Prince of Wales Island, was declared a National Monument. And by 1920, Judge James Wickersham, a man with a great appreciation for Alaska, started a movement to preserve the remaining totems at Port Tongass. Unfortunately, during a 1923 presidential visit to Alaska, Wickersham failed to have President Harding's itinerary revised. Subsequently, the Lincoln Totem Pole, a unique totem Wickersham had hoped to obtain funds to preserve, continued to decay for another 16 years.

In 1926, Dr. H. W. Kreiger of the U.S. National Museum inspected houses and totems at Old Kasaan. Though many were beyond repair, he ordered the remaining ones preserved with creosote. At about the same time, through the efforts of General James Gordon Steese, president of the Alaska Road Commission, a few old poles at Sitka were repainted and raised. At Wrangell, Walter Waters experimented with preserving totems by boring holes on top and pouring rock salt into the bores. And trader Ernest Kirberger, who resided at Kake for 45 years, displayed several Tlingit totems in his store until it burned down in 1926. From 1921 to 1934, forester Charles Flory generated masses of paper lamenting the deterioration of Alaska's Native sites, while government officials systematically ignored him.

Totem Renaissance

In 1931, a group of artists, writers, and a few federal government officials decided that Native American handicrafts might enhance self-sufficiency for a poverty-stricken people. Borrowing archival pieces from museums across the United States, patron Amelia Elizabeth White and artist John Sloan privately funded an Exposition of Indian Arts in New York. Prominent art critics were invited to critique and thus legitimize Native American art.

The idea spread, and in 1934, as part of Roosevelt's New Deal, the Indian Arts and Crafts Board (IACB) was formed with the intention of encouraging the public to buy Native American art works. In 1938, impressed with the U.S. Indian School at Ketchikan, the Sheldon Jackson School at Sitka, and souvenir

**During ceremonies in Metlakatla, esteemed Tsimshian elders in regalia
are seated on this bench emblazoned with community crests.**

totem poles, the IACB arranged a visit for board manager Rene d'Harnoncourt.
His Alaska tour culminated in two well-received exhibitions in San Francisco
and New York, each arranged around a dramatically illuminated 50-foot totem
pole. The invited feature celebrities were Haida elder John Wallace, who had
apprenticed to his carver-father, plus his son, Fred. They performed dances for
audiences and carved additional poles, two of which stand today at New York's
Museum of Modern Art.

Throughout the 1930s and 1940s, magazine writers, interior decorators,
fashion designers, and jewelry makers were actively encouraged to prod the
public into emulating the style and colors favored by American Indian peoples.
The so-called "Lodge Look" emerged, complete with rustic Indian-made accessories to recall the feeling of summer camp spent by a lake or winters at a
mountain retreat. Cherokee, Ojibwa, and Seminole carvers began to carve
souvenir totem poles despite the fact that the totem tradition was unprece-
dented among their people. These efforts produced a jumble of perceptions
about Indians in the public's mind. Teepees and totem poles mixed with feather

hcaddresses, buffalo herds, peace pipes, and Southwest pottery. As the lore of totems mixed with these new "pop" icons, totem poles became a symbol, not just for Alaska, but for all North American Original Peoples.

In April 1933, President Roosevelt approved formation of the Indian Civilian Conservation Corps (CCC) to improve reservation lands. By 1938, in Alaska, forester B. Frank Heintzleman, director of the CCC, was collecting forgotten totems. Of all that remained standing, about 200 were harvested. Linn A. Forrest, a well-known national lodge architect, helped resurrect old clan house designs. Eventually CCC funds of about $200,000 were gathered and nearly 250 Native carvers began to replicate old totem poles and clan houses. With the economic depression in full swing, people searched out nearly eroded totem poles for copying, and rediscovered how to make adzes and other handmade carving tools. After initially confusing traditional colors, samples of the original paints were analyzed, and modern paints were mixed. While woodworking and painting skills were emphasized, supervisors did little

Tlingit men work on duplicating an old totem at Saxman, a project sponsored by the Civilian Conservation Corps in 1939.

however to research the apprentice system, the dances, songs, or ceremonies that were vital to the tradition.

Eventually, teams of workers replicated several ancient poles on the verge of being lost forever, and several more poles were re-carved from memory. "At least 150 of the old poles have been restored or copied, and new ones have been designed," wrote anthropologist Viola Garfield in 1944. Fragments of old poles had been laid beside freshly cut cedar logs, and good-hearted attempts made to replicate them. According to forester Harry Spalding, "The poles are being restored with faithful historical accuracy. . . . " Others disagreed. After traveling to many Pacific Northwest and Alaska totem sites beginning in 1946, writer Edward Malin argued that "the results . . . are an affront to the past. . . ." Nonetheless, totem poles that might have rotted away at that time are instead available for modern viewers to enjoy. Today the results of the CCC intervention are displayed in popular totem parks in Ketchikan (at Saxman and Totem Bight), Sitka National Historic Park, Wrangell, Hydaburg, Kasaan, and Klawock.

The Tradition Evolves

Quietly in Haines, Alaska, beginning in 1947, German immigrant Carl Heinmiller formed a friendship with Mildred Sparks, a respected tribal elder. Using a local Boy Scout troop for practice, Heinmiller and several other enthusiasts began to resurrect the lost dances of the local Tlingit people. And, in August 1952, though the dancers' masks, headdresses, and other regalia were in need of repair, the public enthusiastically embraced the opportunity to once again witness an authentic Tlingit ceremonial dance. This event, repeated throughout Southeast Alaska over the next few decades, culminated in the founding of Alaska Indian Arts, Inc., a program of woodcarving and costume making, the construction of an authentic tribal house, and the 1957 founding of the renowned Chilkat Dancers in Haines. Combining the ideas of Native and non-Native enthusiasts alike, towns like Haines set the stage not only for reviving totem carving but for resurrecting the old songs, dances, and ceremonies that go with the tradition.

Throughout the 1960s and 1970s, small groups of serious carvers were slowly emerging. They set out to revive traditional ways. Many traveled to the location of their patriarchal totems, researched museum collections, and finally

David R. Boxley is among the latest generation of Tsimshian carvers.

collaborated with each other. They practiced their skills, verified their traditions, and began to teach others the ancient styles of Pacific Northwest Coast art. One old master carver, Mungo Martin, a Kwakiutl artist who had carved in secret for many years, set up an open workshop behind the Provincial Museum in Victoria, B.C., in 1952. There he inspired dozens of apprentices from throughout the Pacific Northwest and Alaska. Next emerged two notable contributors to the totem renaissance, art historian Bill Holm in Seattle and Haida master carver Bill Reid in Vancouver, B.C.

At the 1964 World's Fair in New York, the igloo-shaped Alaska Pavilion was fronted with the three well traveled 30 foot totems originally carved for the 1904 St. Louis World's Fair. By 1969, Alaska Indian Arts, Inc. in Haines had produced the world's largest totem pole to date via the work of pioneering carvers Edwin Kasko, Carl Heinmiller, Jenny Lyn Smith, Warren Price, and Leo Jacobs Sr. And at the Alaska Pavilion for the 1970 World's Fair in Japan, villagers from Kake built what still may be the world's tallest properly sanctioned totem pole.

Throughout the 1970s, the Department of the Interior Indian Arts and Crafts Board sponsored workshops for Tlingit and Haida carvers. The apprentice system was revived at the Totem Heritage Center in Ketchikan, culminating in offering the prestigious Certificate of Merit in Carving. The apprentice system was also instituted at the Southeast Alaska Cultural Center in Sitka. Led by a few gifted artists, a new standard of totem art found its way into Alaska's ferry terminals, government buildings, private collections, and galleries. Master carvers such as David Svenson, Greg Horner, Wayne Price, and John

Hagen began their careers during this period. For over 30 years, they have not only been woodcarving, but also working with materials such as silver, gold, and glass. Ketchikan's Totem Heritage Center was established in 1976 to house a priceless collection of old totem fragments, and in Sitka, the National Park Service provided funding for the carving of eight new poles between 1978 and 1986. Carving the first pole cost $4,000, the last $22,000.

Famed Alaska carver Nathan Jackson progressed from creating pocketknife carvings with his clan relative Ted Lawrence in the 1950s through an initiation period visiting museum totem collections in New York, attending the Santa Fe School of Indian Art, and dancing and carving with Haines's Carl Heinmiller of Alaska Indian Arts, Inc. Jackson shared in Alaska State Museum kudos with carver Tony Hunt in 1971, shared expertise with carver Duane Pasco, and learned adz skills as well as design fundamentals from art historian Bill Holm. Through these sorts of efforts and more, talented Natives throughout the Pacific Northwest and Alaska were able to relearn traditional forms of Native carving and its attendant ceremonies. Consequently, over the past half century, both the quality of totem art and the amount being distributed has greatly increased.

Tlingit carver Frank Fulmer accompanies his mother to Glacier Bay, her family's ancient hunting area.

Throughout the 1980s and 1990s, an increasing number of talented carvers developed both respect and affinity for the traditional art forms. Old poles retrieved from museums were carefully restored; new poles were carved for parks and collectors. Alaska steadily produced a number of talented carvers, including David A. Boxley and his son David R. Boxley, Bruce Cook, Will

Burkhart, Darald DeWitt, Frank L. Fulmer, John Hagen, Greg Horner, Joe Jacobs, Nathan Jackson and his son Stephen Jackson, Israel Shotridge and his brother Norman G. Jackson, Ernest Smeltzer, and Lee Wallace.

Then in August 2001, under a blazing-hot sun, invited guests gathered at the Pilchuck Glass School in Washington state, famous for founder-glassmaker Dale Chihuly. There they witnessed the raising of the first totem to combine traditional red cedar with cast, etched, and blown glass components, along with the use of neon lighting. Alaska master carvers John Hagen, David Svenson, and others, collaborating with Tlingit glass artist Preston Singletary, raised *The Founders Totem Pole*, thus bridging tradition and innovation.

Over the last 50 years, non-Natives also have become increasingly recognized for their contributions, whether it be in original Native-style art, conducting classes or workshops, giving lectures, or writing articles and books. Academics such as Robin K. Wright, art historian and curator of the Burke Museum in Seattle, represent a long line of caring individuals who have sought to document and preserve totem traditions.

And so totem lore grows. In the Native village of Saxman near Ketchikan, a daily parade of tourists files by a stand of totem poles, some 30 and 40 feet tall. In a shed nearby, Tlingit master carver Nathan Jackson, who has been designated a National Living Treasure, wields an adz of Swedish steel. With each swing of his arm, a cedar shaving the size of a fingernail flies off. Jackson works on the totem, detailing exquisite features into a figure that will sit 30 feet above the ground. Despite the modern country music pulsating from the radio in his workshop, the technique of carving totems remains unchanged. He patiently answers questions. As a person who has guided emerging carvers for over 30 years, Jackson wants his apprentices to develop an appreciation for their cultural traditions, and pass them on to their children and grandchildren. Jackson has studied older poles and learned much from early carvers.

"It's too bad we didn't get to see or talk to any of these guys," he says, "because they were pretty good themselves. It'd be dandy to get a critique here or there." Yes, it would be good to hear from them. While their exact words may be lost in time, their wisdom lives on in Alaska's totem tradition. ■

3

Totem Crest Figures

Carving Styles

From early times, there have been differences among the totem art styles of Southeast Alaska Native tribes. Traditional Haida crests, for example, were tightly interlocked in a cylindrical fashion around a pole, with creatures biting one another, grasping a fin, thrusting a tongue, or squatting between the legs or ears of another creature. Beaks or snouts were flattened into a pole's surface. The Haida were noted for their natural representation of human faces, with generously sized eyes formed with two pointed sides. Pole top eyes focused downward, while lower figures peered straight ahead at the viewer.

By contrast, ancient Tlingit totem makers carved figures that stood separately from each other, with wings, fins, beaks, and snouts outlined in paint or carved as wood additions. Circular eye pupils gazed blankly into space. In the late 1600s, Tlingit totem carvers came into contact with the Kaigani Haida, who had recently arrived in a large migration. As the two cultures intermingled, Tlingit totem figures began to take on some features of the Haida style.

On this Tlingit totem in Hoonah, a smug Raven stands beneath one eye of an Octopus and below Wolf with its shell teeth.

Tsimshian "uninvited guest" (left) in a Metlakatla pole holds a funeral basket of roses. In an ancient Haida pole, a bearded figure (right) probably ridicules a non-Native man.

Back in Canada, the Tsimshian people of the Nass and Skeena Rivers in British Columbia also came into contact with the Haida people, and were influenced in some ways by their powerful style. Tsimshian tradition was revived in Alaska in the 1970s, when culture bearers arrived to teach songs, dancing, and carving.

All three tribes have liberally borrowed from each other's stories, and added new human figures to their collection of animal crests. The Haida may have been the first to depict the Watchmen, three tiny crouched men wearing *skils*—distinctive hats topped by ringed sections. Each hat segment symbolized a potlatch the owner had hosted, and the Watchmen kept an unending lookout for danger. Reflecting this hat form, some Tlingit and Tsimshian totem poles came to have a large blank section with segments carved into it. The taller the unornamented part of the totem, the greater the prestige of its owner.

Today the three tribal groups still have distinct traditional style differences, and with study, the viewer can come to understand the different styles. But in the last half century, up and down the Pacific Northwest Coast, there also has been a burgeoning of new, personalized styles coming out of a strong awareness of traditional styles, as individual Native carvers find their own aesthetic directions.

Color on Totems

Since the earliest explorers arrived, it was noted that some totem poles had applied colors while others did not. Presumably a man with an eye for color, French explorer Capt. Etienne Marchand reported that the totems he saw in 1791 were of a "vibrant red, black, and apple green"—a remarkably precise description for that era. Today, whether a totem has color or not is a decision made by the carver and the tradition he is following. Certain carvers leave the carved cedar trunk unpainted, allowing it to transform to a natural silver gray color, just as human hair does. Others paint on a few highlights, while still others paint every available surface.

Traditionally, the pigments used for totem poles were limited to hues of red, black, or blue green. Traditional colors appeared as semitransparent stains rather than opaque paints. Red ochre, a naturally occurring iron oxide mineral

---

Rare old Tlingit totem (left) in Wrangell was colored with natural semitransparent stains. Modern Tlingit totem in Ketchikan (right) was painted with house paint.

rock, was crushed to form red powder. Urine mixed with crushed copper nodules made blue green, and burned hemlock bark ground with charcoal bits made black. To create bonding agents for these colors, the powders were blended with salmon eggs, salty seawater, seal liver bile, and large quantities of saliva. The resting mucilage was mixed with melted seal grease and applied as a paste, or warmed and applied in liquid form as heated tallow. Two rare examples of early stained totems are on display inside Chief Shakes's house in Wrangell. Ever since carvers could barter with a ship's carpenter, colors have been applied using regular house paint.

Among today's Haida, Tlingit, and Tsimshian carvers, almost all of them paint at least the basic highlights—eyes, eyebrows, mouths, and noses. They may leave the background unpainted or paint the entire pole. It's according to personal preference, says Tsimshian carver David A. Boxley. Painted totem poles need regular maintenance to keep colored surfaces bright, though old totems with fading colors have a certain charm. On totems that are painted, black is applied to the primary outlines, red is for secondary elements, and blue or blue green for tertiary areas. Individual carvers may add sienna, yellow, white, brown, green, or light blue. Apple green is rare. Despite several color theories advanced by fanciful folks with wild imaginations, most totem-makers practice down-to-earth logic. Teeth are painted white, animal furs are brown, claws are black, tongues are red, and eyes are white with black centers. There are a few conventions: octopus parts are red—the creature's favorite color—and a red nose indicates stinginess. Mythical creatures such as Thunderbird and Sea Wolf display a wide range of colors, for who is to say what their true colors really are.

Totem Realities

Family groups, or clans, officially acquired new crests when certain conditions were met. Crests were obtained through intermarriage, as payment for a debt or restitution for a crime, if a defeated chief passed on his rights to certain crests, or if a heroic person returned from a supernatural encounter possessing authorized crests accepted as legal by the shaman and the tribe.

For the Pacific Northwest Coast Indians, in a time not long ago there was a parallel reality superimposed upon the world in which ordinary humans dwell. Without realizing it, a human might step into or out of this world. Or during a hunt, a human might slay an animal from this alternate existence, put on its skin,

In this Tlingit totem, the crouching man's hat may symbolize his journey into the spirit realm.

and gain supernatural powers. The alternate reality, existing within three realms—the sky world, underwater world, and land world—seemed strangely like home. But the creatures were old-fashioned, living life as humans did before contact. In this place, transformation is a key power. Spirit-creatures had the ability to turn into humans, into other animals, or even into objects such as pine needles or rocks. Time was distorted and the dead didn't always remain dead. Ordinary people lost their fears, had the ability to cure other's wounds and illnesses, could be instantly transported to different areas, and became quite attached to the supernatural residents who lived there. Once trapped there, a human began to forget his or her ordinary life. If the human did manage to return home, he or she became a hero with authorized crests that were then passed on to descendants and displayed on their totem poles.

Some of the crests listed below are widely used among the Tlingit, Haida, and Tsimshian peoples; others are lesser crests appearing occasionally. Alaska's most common totem crest figures are discussed.

Totem Crests

BEAR AND BEAR MOTHER. Bear is a widely used crest figure usually recognized by its sharp teeth, somewhat pointed snout, large round nostrils, and flat-topped ears. Sometimes the figure is Bear Mother; she may hold one or both of her twin cubs in her paws or perhaps within her eyes or ears. She or her cubs can also confusingly appear as humans. Also known as Xóots, Kaiti, or Grizzly, Bear may be depicted squatting on its haunches, or in full animal profile sitting horizontally on top of a shaft sometimes incised with bear claw

Bear (left) in Juneau with sharp incisor teeth displays distinctive Tlingit blue-green color. Tlingit Beaver at Saxman Totem Park (right) holds its crosshatched tail.

marks. The subject of several stories, Bear interacts enthusiastically with humans, has a special affinity for pretty human princesses, often becoming the ancestor of a human Bear clan.

BEAVER. In earlier times, only those with rights to engage in the lucrative fur trade displayed Beaver crests. With two bucked teeth in front, its tail cross-hatched and displayed in the front of the animal, Beaver sometimes holds a stick or arrow between its two front paws. If the arrow is broken, it symbolizes peace after a war. Considered malicious creatures that could chisel murderous arrows, Beavers were noted for tunneling under villages or slapping their huge tails to cause earthquakes or landslides. The Killisnoo Beaver has a magical tail with a face on it that must be killed separately if a person wants this Beaver to die. Called Tsing by the Haida, by merely chanting a song Beaver could change snowy weather into warm misty rain. Also in Haida stories, Beaver was once one of Raven's uncles, who long ago lived on the floor of the sea where he hoarded all the fresh water and fish of the world.

BLACKFISH, OR KILLER WHALE. Recognized on totems by its dark fish-shaped body, dorsal fin, and blowhole, Killer Whale, an important Tsimshian crest, is found on the totems of all Southeast Alaska Native groups. A famous Alaska chief once conquered a tribe in British Columbia that considered Killer Whale their most important crest. Rather than endure life as a slave, the defeated chief gave up his clan rights to the figure. Since then, Killer Whale has appeared head-down signaling defeat among the people who lost the battle, while a horizontal or heads-up posture indicates victory.

In the spirit world, the Killer Whale people, also known as Blackfish or Orca, live in underwater villages, where they fraternize with a number of powerful underwater characters including Copper Woman and Komogwa, the

THE ORIGIN OF KILLER WHALE

The skilled hunter Naatsilanéi once went spear fishing with his ever-jealous brothers-in-law. In spite of the protestations of the youngest, his resentful in-laws purposely abandoned him, silently gliding off in their dugout canoe. Finding himself alone, Naatsilanéi administered first aid to an ailing sea gull, who gratefully introduced him to the Sea Lions. In their underwater village, he spotted the chief's son, ailing from the very wound that Naatsilanéi had inflicted on him earlier that day. In return for healing his son, the Sea Lion Chief presented Naatsilanéi with the gift of an inflatable sea lion skin. Crawling inside, our hero floated back to his village and cunningly crept home for his tools. Back on the beach, he carved eight Killer Whales figures, first from alder, then spruce, then hemlock. But when he carved them from yellow cedar, they drifted out to sea, animated into living Whales, and returned with fish for him. Thus fortified, he instructed the Whales to kill his brothers-in-law, save for the youngest, which they did. After this nasty deed, Naatsilanéi instructed them to never again harm humans. This they mostly obeyed, although because of their yellow cedar origins, whale fat crackles in a fire just like wood.

(Enthnographer Barbeau attributes one version of this story to anthropologist Viola E. Garfield, who collected it in the 1930s regarding a totem at the village of Tuxekan, Alaska. Throughout the 1920s and 1930s, H. P. Corser, a Member of the American School of Archeology, collected totem stories throughout Alaska. Walter C. Waters, the owner of a store in Wrangell published several of Corser's stories, including this one, in 1940.) ●

Undersea King. Killer Whale can capture a canoe, drag it under water, and transform its occupants into Killer Whales. Sometimes, a Killer Whale near the shore is a transformed human, trying to communicate with his family. Rare totems display the crests of the mythic Double- or Triple-finned Killer Whale. Nanasimget, a mere human, appears on several Killer Whale totems; his story tells of a man who once rode a Killer Whale to its underwater domain desperately seeking his kidnapped wife.

EAGLE, THUNDERBIRD, AND OTHER RAPTORS. On totems, raptors are recognizable as birds with prominent hooked beaks. Eagle is a common crest in Alaska. The Haida, Tsimshian, and Tlingit first called these creatures Eagle, while in the past century the use of the term "Thunderbird" seems to have crept in from the desert dwellers of the American Southwest. Eagle is notable as a totem-topper, but can appear elsewhere, anywhere from a totem's midsection upward.

Only a few humans have ever made it to the spirit sky realm where Eagle lives. A flock of geese, acting like helium balloons, have flown a few lucky Tsimshian up to where Eagle and Thunderbird rule. But others who wish to commune with these gigantic raptors have climbed high into the mountains to wait for a thunderstorm to sweep them up into the sky kingdom. Some say lightning is produced as Thunderbird blinks its angry golden eyes; others say it's a dart from Thunderbird's serpentlike tongue. Thunder is said to originate from the beating of its enormous wings.

In general, Eagle is preoccupied with its own sky wars and ignores humans, though once during a terrible plague, a certain Mother Eagle brought fish to a starving girl and her grandmother. When it feels hungry, Eagle pulls on a cloak of feathers and searches for Whales or Giant Woodworms, its favorite foods. Female eagles are said to bring bad luck to any human who mocks their overly thick feather leggings. It is rumored that these raptors will lift roof beams into place for their favorite clansmen, while others claim benefits such as exceptional eyesight from owning an eagle feather. As well as being an important clan crest among Southeast Alaska tribes, eagles were liberally depicted on the official coats of arms of Imperial Russia, Great Britain, Germany, and the United States. And so various totem carvers have used Eagle to represent many nations.

Also living in the sky villages is Hawk, a raptor with a bluntly curved beak and a taste for eating Mosquito. Favored on mortuary poles, Hawk is a rare crest

An Eagle at Totem Bight Historical State Park has its eyes fixed on the realm of the sky world, which, according to Tlingit stories, preoccupies the bird.

but an invaluable guardian spirit. Occasionally Hawk Woman, an elusive young woman with a hawklike beak, will assist humans too.

The legendary and powerful Kadjuk, perched atop a tall pole, is a huge eaglelike raptor found only in Alaska. The undecorated portion of the pole symbolizes the lofty habitat of this bird and the high esteem in which the crest is held. Kadjuk amuses itself by dropping stones on unsuspecting groundhogs. If a human is lucky enough to acquire one of these stones, his or her prosperity is assured for all time.

FROG. This little green creature is an important and lucky crest. Frog may appear alone on a totem, emerging from the mouth or ears of another creature, or wedged between other forms. Frog is easy to identify. Looking like its animal counterpart, with its broad toothless mouth, big eyes, and crouched position, Frog has the power to explode and then reconstitute itself. People who underestimate Frog's power find themselves dead. Frog has friends in high places, is linked with volcanoes or fire and with acquiring wealth—especially in the form of copper. It was once said that Frog could survive being buried in lava, and that was why copper could be found near old eruption sites.

Frog is a common crest of an ancient and fruitful lineage, and as such the bare breasts of some female crest figures are rendered as two Frogs. Haida people carve Frog onto house poles to keep the house strong, while Flying Frog is a rare crest depicted as a protector in front of a shaman's house. In Haida stories, a vengeful Frog sits on the handle of a staff carried by Dzelarhons, the Frog clan princess. On one Saxman Park totem, Frog heads peek up from receding lake waters. And on a famous ridicule totem pole in Wrangell, three Frogs represent the clan designations of the three people being humiliated.

HEROES AND HEROINES. Humans may be woven among totem animal figures or appear on their own. They are considered story figures or minor crests. Depicted with a *skils* or ringed potlatch hat, humans of high rank snuggle within an animal crest's paws or between its legs. A chief wearing a huge ceremonial hat

SOOTY SKIN, OR DUK-TOOTHL

A huge Sea Lion had killed the best hunter in the village. Seeking revenge, the deceased hunter's uncles organized a plan. All their nephews were to go into training. The young men were required to bathe in cold saltwater and beat themselves with branches to build up their endurance. But one nephew refused to train. Thought to be lazy, he was normally curled up asleep in the ashes beside the fire. Soon he was scorned for his sooty skin and mockingly called Duk-toothl. At night, however, this young man secretly built up his strength and learned to hold his breath underwater. The day of the contest, the nephews prepared for battle. Because everyone belittled him, Duk-toothl had to beg to attend. After all the young men have failed, our hero dove underwater, chased a sea lion, captured it, then ripped it in half. Those who were cruel to him were now fearful of the boy's strength. Duk-toothl did not take revenge on his tormentors, but instead forgave them, thus showing his strength of character, as well as of body.

Historic totem with human hair shows Duk-toothl tearing a sea lion in half.

(First collected by anthropologist J. R. Swanton about 1910 and published in *Tlingit Myths and Texts*, author Edward L. Keithahn again collected this Tlingit story in Wrangell, and published it in 1946. Marius Barbeau repeated it in his book, *Totem Poles*, published in 1950.) •

A Tlingit girl in a Ketchikan pole appears under Sun and above a figure (probably Moon) on Raven's hat.

that is formed from the body of a Whale or a Bear represents victory. His vanquished enemies are from the clan whose hat he is wearing. Appearing on totems in threes with tall potlatch hats, Village Watchmen do guard-duty, while Master Carver holding his adz is a hero with obvious talent. Kats, a story figure and Tlingit hunter, is a man who has supernatural encounters with Bear, while Kayak, another Tlingit boy from stories, receives a magical canoe and a harpoon before encountering a one-legged fisherman and several sea monsters. Sooty Skin, the strongman, also known as Blackskin or Duk-toothl is an important crest and exclusive to Alaska.

Human females in traditional dress are considered minor totem figures but are particularly striking crests on totems throughout Alaska. Considered the vessels that hold human history, women in woven cedar garments and holding salmon appear on several modern totem poles. On one totem in Metlakatla, a beautiful woman holding a bunch of roses is called the "Uninvited Guest." She represents death, a most unwelcome visitor to those who cannot overcome their addictions.

INANIMATE FORMS. Figures such as the Sun, Moon, Stars, or Rainbow are sometimes featured as minor totem crests, though more often they are seen carved on masks. Sun is a face with rays, while Moon is a round face without rays. An eclipse of Moon is depicted as Codfish trying to swallow the Moon. Rainbow is a rare crest, sometimes appearing on top of a totem with a human holding it aloft. Rarely seen crests include South Wind and North Wind, Fireweed, and Sundog, which are usually portrayed as human figures. The figure of Mountain Man with a triangular headpiece appears personified on top of a totem pole in Juneau and on another in Wrangell.

LAND MONSTERS. Left over from a time long ago when cannibals ruled the world, fearsome Monsters have frightening stories and are minor crests. Of the so-called Wild Men, the thick-skinned Goo-teekhl and Gootz-hun—appearing as ferocious human figures—are ancient crests whose stories are lost. When a cannibal or Wild Man is burned, its ashes fly up into the air to be transformed into little gray insects with a taste for blood. With its pointy proboscis, Mosquito, a monsterlike crest on some totems, is the result.

The Kooshdaaḵáa, Gagixit, or Land Otter People are some sort of Bigfoot or Sasquatch ape creatures appearing as giant humans covered in otter fur skin. Alternately they can appear exactly like their namesake, normal otters. However they have the ability to make themselves invisible, and have a yen to kidnap humans. Years later their pathetic victims can only grovel about on their hands and knees. Kooshdaaḵáas are creatures that can transform into an insect, then stealthily bore into a person who is sleeping.

Woodworm, also known as Scrubworm or Grubworm, an out-of-control pet, is depicted as a giant segmented worm. After an innocent girl befriends one and secretly feeds it cooking oil, it threatens to devour her entire village. To destroy it, the mighty Thunderbird is summoned.

LOON. Depicted not as a bird, but as a woman with bird features, Loon grants women great skill in weaving. The men who display this crest become fine fishermen. As the fog rolls in, this melancholy sounding bird delights in frightening humans on the shore or in their canoes.

MINK. Another rare crest, Mink resembles its fur-bearing animal counterpart. Considered mischievous and one of Raven's closest associates, Mink acts as the arranger for some of Raven's most dubious schemes.

OTTER. Once when Raven was traveling the world, he came across a man sharpening a spear with which to kill him. He turned the man into Otter and the spear became its tail. Otter, which looks like its land animal counterpart and is not to be confused with the fearsome Land Otter people, was once an ancient

Haida crest, but the people who were authorized to use it all perished in various plagues. Today, Otter is slowly being revived.

OWL. A relatively rare crest once viewed as the frightening carrier of unfortunate news, Owl is enjoying a surge in popularity among today's totem pole carvers. Resembling a barn owl with its tightly curled beak, Owl is a figure that once lived on the earth as a man or a woman with in-law problems. A person who catches an Owl at twilight while it is in the act of turning day into night can claim Owl as a crest—though the person must first escape turning into an Owl. With their special power of prophecy and as the guardian of shamans, Owl is credited with bringing back messages from the recently departed.

RAVEN. A legendary creature, Raven is a significant Alaska crest, a powerful trickster who appears in dozens of traditional stories. A mischievous bird spirit

RAVEN LIBERATES THE SUN, MOON, AND STARS

Raven was going along one day when he spied a great clan house and a beautiful girl beside it. She was drawing water. This was in the time before-now when there were no stars or planets, no tides or animals as we know them, and it was twilight all the time. Wandering around after having recently burned himself black in a fire and hungry as usual, he was restless. But the girl's father knew of clever Raven, so his house was closely guarded. Crafty Raven therefore transformed himself into a pine needle ready to float down the stream. When the girl next came to

Mischievous Raven tops this Tlingit pole.

fetch water, she took a drink and swallowed the pine needle. She soon gave birth to a precocious son who ate constantly and shrieked mercilessly. He begged for the bentwood box full of twinkling stars hidden in the corner. When the stars flew up ➤

depicted frequently on dozens of totems in Alaska, he has a prominent long, blunt beak, and is credited with causing every known phenomenon in nature. Also known as Yalth, Gaanaxadi, We-gyet, or Txamsem, bawdy Raven is so powerful he occasionally appears on totems with symbols of nobility such as a Chilkat blanket or a *skils* hat. Though he maliciously breaks the rules of nature, Raven's impish antics prove to have beneficial effects for ordinary humans. On at least a dozen Alaskan totems, Raven appears with Sun or stands on the bentwood box from which he liberated the Sun, the light of the world.

Raven lives in the sky realm along with his slaves Gitsanuk and Gitsaqeq, though he is often found greedily begging for food or shiny objects somewhere on Earth. Ever curious and naughty, he has led his people to new homelands and founded an important family clan. Some claim he has a brother named Logobola. Once, when Logobola flew over the earth, he splashed around the

RAVEN LIBERATES THE SUN, MOON, AND STARS continued

the smoke hole, he pretended to be sorry. Next he demanded the silvery Moon that hung on the wall, and though his grandfather objected, his mother gave in. Flicking the Moon up through the smoke hole, it flew into the sky while Raven screeched in delight. Next he whined for the box his grandfather kept hidden under his bed. Day after day, he would not stop complaining until his mother relented, planning to guard it closely. Quickly Raven threw himself and the box into the fire, escaped on the updraft, and resumed his bird form.

"Fetch me some food and drink," he demanded of everyone he met, "for I own something wonderful." But they mocked him. With a thundering flash he threw open the box, and the Sun flew into the heavens. Those who were wearing animal skins became animals forevermore, and those who were naked became humans. And that is how sun, moon, and stars came to be in the heavens.

(In the 1870s, carver Albert Edward Edenshaw related this Raven story to accompany a totem he made for the Haida, though both the Tlingit and Tsimshian traditions claim many early Raven stories. Early ethnographers and anthropologists collected this rendition several more times: Franz Boas in 1902, J. R. Swanton about 1910, William Benyon in 1922, and Edward L. Keithahn, circa 1930. Marius Barbeau included it in his 1950 book, *Totem Poles*, attributing one version to an old Haida sea captain, Andrew Brown, who told this now-familiar version to him in 1939.) ●

water he was carrying. It fell to the ground and turned into Alaska's freshwater streams and lakes. Therefore, Logobola is responsible when there is a lack of water in Alaska.

SEA MONSTERS. Ocean-living monsters with warlike qualities are some of Alaska's most legendary crest figures. Particularly exciting sea monster crests are composed of two creatures morphed into one. The rare Sea Bear, with its alternating whale features and bear parts, has fewer powers than more common Sea Wolf, also known as Wasgo, a creature who brings luck to all who can spot one. Gonakadet (or Gonadet or Gunakade) is another name for Wasgo, and it's sometimes called Old Witch of the Sea. Though Sea Wolf usually appears with a combination of wolf paws and killer whale fins, it has several more unusual transformations. Furiously shedding water droplets, Sea Wolf can sport coppery winglike appendages, or suddenly rise from the sea as a threatening humanlike witch. It can mysteriously appear as an elaborately painted war canoe, or even as a beautifully painted house, inlaid with blue and green shells and topped with the head of an immense fish. Both American and German submarine corps have been inspired by this stealthy Alaska totem creature—the mythic Sea Wolf.

SPIRIT WOMEN. Fog Woman, also known as Bright-Cloud Woman, is a totem story figure often depicted with a saucer-shaped hat and recognized as a human woman with a labret or lip plug—a symbol of aristocracy. Though she was briefly married to the great and powerful Raven, she left him because he was such a poor provider. But before she departed, she first learned a powerful skill. Forced to beg for herself and her daughters, she discovered that upon turning her magical spruce-root hat upside down, all the fogs and mists would enter it, leaving the sky clear and bright. Fog Woman's daughters, the Creek Women, are beauties, depicted as human girls, who live at the head of every stream and protect the salmon. It is the ultimate joy of a salmon's life to fight its way upstream for one look at these lovely young women.

Perhaps the record number of names held by one character goes to the magnificent Haida noblewoman, Djilaqons (or Dzelarhons), Princess of Frogs and spirit protector of the Eagle clan. In various wardrobe changes, she is depicted as a beautiful woman usually with some sort of Frog components in her garb or on the top of a cane she uses. She is variously known as

Volcano Woman, Copper Woman, Property Woman, or Wealth Woman. Needless to say she brings good luck and prosperity. In stories she is an ambitious socialite, friend of Frog, and married either to the noble Prince of Bears or to Komogwa, the underwater king who smelts copper. She's far different from the vengeful Foam Woman, a whirlpool monster depicted as a devouring woman with a big mouth, feared by warriors even when they are paddling in their sturdiest war canoes. And going about her daily business is Old Woman of the Tides, a cranky foe of Raven, depicted as a woman covered in spiny urchins because of Raven, who delights in throwing sea urchins at her buttocks.

A contemporary Tlingit pole near Ketchikan's Totem Heritage Center depicts a woman of distinction.

UNDERWATER ANIMALS. Bullhead, a fishlike figure with whiskers, appears in several Raven stories and on a few totem poles. Beginning as a beautiful white fish and outwitted by Raven, it ends up as a skinny, bony creature. Sculpin, an ancient totem crest, takes its name from a tiny fish found in Alaskan waters. Recognizable for its flat spikes, the sculpin fish's pointy bones were traditionally made into armor plate. In stories, any human who pressed into these spines suffered horribly. At Sitka one pole depicts a flawed human, the incestuous Lakich'inei, with one of his children, who is half-human and half-dog. Pressing the child against his coat made from a Sculpin spine, the child dies.

Devilfish is the frightening name given to Octopus, a crest easily recognizable by its red color, eight legs, and suckered tentacles. Whole villages of Octopus people live under the sea, are reputed to love the color red, and lie in wait for unsuspecting humans, especially those who harm their babies. This denizen of the deep delights in pulling its prey down slowly into the watery brine, though occasionally it merely kidnaps a person, stealing him or her away to live with the Octopus people. Giant Rock Oyster and Clam, depicted only as menacing faces on totem poles, also choose to trap humans, usually by the arm, drowning them slowly as the tide turns. Today, these figures-that-slowly-drown-humans are said to be a metaphor for vice.

Dogfish, also known as Shark, or Mud Shark, is an uncommon but particularly striking crest that is depicted on utilitarian household objects and a few totem poles. It has a flat look and crescent-shaped gill slits. Dogfish is often portrayed with a labret inserted in its lip, the reminder of a noblewoman who Dogfish carried off long ago. On Haida totems, she is Dogfish Woman, an upper-class woman with a labret, gill slits on her forehead and a prim crown, a shape-changing creature who is part human and part shark. A rarely obtained spirit, those who gain Shark's favor sing chants and become skillful dancers.

Halibut is depicted as a flatfish and is recognized by both eyes being on the upper side of its body. The Tlingit say some of the outlying islands took their present shape when Halibut grew to an enormous size and broke up into

At Saxman near Ketchikan, Giant Rock Oyster holds the unfortunate Tlingit person who dared taunt him.

little islands. The crashing of its tail scattered people all around. The powerful Prince of Halibut appears in a few stories. Salmon beings live in underwater villages though they seem to retain their fishlike personalities even when encountering humans. If a human eats a Salmon underwater, its bones immediately reassemble and it swims away. A figure holding a shrimp or a crab in its mouth is significant in Haida culture; both are regarded as symbols of thievery.

GONAKADET, THE SEA WOLF

A Tlingit man once loved his dear wife, but his mother-in-law was constantly berating him for his failures as a hunter. One day, he spotted Gonakadet, a fearsome Sea Wolf known to bring luck. Cunningly trapping and skinning the creature, he donned its skin. Thus garbed, he could not be recognized. Unwilling to tell lest his enemies steal the skin, he wore it fishing. Not only did our hero catch a fish for his wife, he secretly left a huge fish as a gift for his mother-in-law. She was delighted, but not knowing who had given her the gift, continued to criticize him for sleeping all day. The next night he left her two more fish, then three, then four, and so on. Soon the mother-in-law claimed she was divine and could predict how many fish would appear. Morning after morning, the household stood amazed as ever-greater quantities of fish appeared. Everyone in the household was well fed. In time, she bragged that she would be gifted with a whale. By now, our hero was exhausted. He took his wife aside to tell her, "If you find something peculiar, be kind." Next morning, intermingled with the dead whale was a strange monster with copper claws, a big head, two fins, and a curly tail. The wife peeked inside the monster's mouth and spotted her husband. She scooped up his body and the skin, and took them to a secret location. No more fish or whales appeared and the villagers turned on the old woman. "Your bragging killed our savior," they complained, and she was shamed to death. His grieving wife put the dry, cracking skin into the lake, and it reanimated. "Onto my back," her transformed husband cried. And the two of them lived forever in a beautiful house with the Daughters of Creeks.

(Journalist James Deans collected a version of this story published in 1889. Anthropologist J. R. Swanton collected a variation in about 1913, as did Edward L. Keithahn around 1946. H. P. Corser, a member of the American School of Archeology, collected totem stories throughout Alaska. Walter C. Waters, the owner of a store in Wrangell, published several of his stories, including this one, in 1940. It continues to be told.) ●

Sea Lion people appear seal-like in shape. Unreliable friends, they either assist humans who have stumbled into the underwater world or kill them mercilessly. After one such murder they were required to make their peace with Duk-toothl, a young man developing his physical strength. To show his prowess he ripped a Sea Lion in half.

WHITE PERSONS. The first President Lincoln figure carved on top of a totem pole came from Tongass Island near Alaska's southern border shortly after the Alaska purchase. The figure resembles the famous president with his stovepipe hat. A small band of Tlingit, seeking sanctuary with a garrison of American soldiers, learned about Lincoln and his efforts to end slavery. In response, a carver named Thele-da produced an amazingly realistic Lincoln for the top of a totem. Since then, Lincoln as the Great Emancipator has appeared on several more totems. One is displayed in Juneau at the Alaska State Museum. Another is at Saxman Totem Village near Ketchikan.

Bearded human figures considered to be white persons appear on a few totems. One has epaulets, buttons, and pockets, suggesting a military person. Some say the eagle crest near this figure is copied from old American coins, while others say it is an Imperial Russian Eagle landing on his head to humiliate him. In another case, the bearded person is a trader the carver decided to ridicule for not paying his debts.

WOLF. Wolf and Raven are the most important crests in southeast Alaska. In spite of this, there are few recorded Wolf stories. Wolf has a longer snout than Bear but the same incisor teeth, and often sits crouched on its haunches. To become a good hunter, one must acquire the power associated with Wolf. Since wolves howl at night, spirit-Wolves are said to attend midnight parties. They also become great drummers and mask-makers, and associate with women who wear bright robes. Reaching under the clothes of these lady companions reveals nothing but bones, for these dancers are Ghost people, who also enjoy Wolf's midnight parties. From these strange companions, Wolf has learned the secrets of healing, though it cannot heal itself. It takes the Tsimshian human hero Gamlugydes to heal the Prince of Wolves. A Wolf crest holder is a good dancer and often a powerful shaman, who can transform himself into a Wolf. ■

4

CHAPTER

Frequently Asked Questions about Totem Poles

What do totems mean? Traditionally, a totem pole portrayed inherited crests signifying the entitlements and rank of a related group of people. Because totems are now also carved for outsiders, totem poles have evolved to represent a combination of traditional elements, Native pride, and whatever the master carver and the owners agree that they represent.

Is it possible to "read" a totem pole? Anyone with an understanding of crests can recognize many totem figures. But it is impossible to fully interpret a totem pole's meaning without knowing the history of the family that owns it.

Were old totems constructed to honor tribal ancestors? No. Old totem poles were primarily a record of an entire clan's kinship status, rights, achievements, and deeds with an occasional heroic migration story indicating how their village came to be in its present location. There were, however, memorial totems for specific individuals that portrayed all his crests.

Were totems worshipped? No. Like a country's flag, they were treated with respect.

This clan house entryway in Wrangell displays a painted Bear that was Tlingit Chief Charles Jones Shakes's clan crest about 1940.

Do totems bring good luck? Totems are neither talismans nor charms. Stealing a totem or owning the tallest totem, however, have both invited misfortune. Tall totems have provoked fights, arguments, firings, murders, pole disfigurements, and official dismantling.

What's the difference between totemism and totem poles? Totemism is a belief that certain qualities imparted to an object, such as a stone in the shape of an animal, can be shared with the human who owns the object. Southwest desert-dwelling Zuni people reflect this tradition in fetishes called "animal totems." Though an Alaska totem can convey goodwill, it does not protect anyone.

Do totem poles have anything to do with Freud's "totem"? Sigmund Freud, father of psychoanalysis, discussed a symbolic object of worship protected by taboos, the "totem," as the representation of hidden guilt within the human psyche. Freud's interpretation has nothing to do with the Alaska totem tradition.

Are totem poles like coats of arms? The coat of arms of the United States, an eagle holding a shield, branch, and arrows, represents America's marks of distinction. Many European families research their surname to discover their ancestors' coat of arms. In the same way, it can be argued that a totem pole is a symbolic system for displaying and recording its owners' distinctions or stories.

Where did the word "totem" originate? Explorers to Alaska in the late 1700s labeled the monument-like wooden poles they saw as "great wooden images," "large tree entrances," "monumental figures," "carved trees," "house posts," and "pillars." The largest number of Native words in use in the English language derived from the Native people who were first encountered by white settlers, the eastern Algonquian tribes. In Ojibwa—an Algonquin language—the expression *ototeman* means roughly "he is a relative of mine." French anthropologist Claude Levi-Strauss speculated that this was the origin of the word. The word, twisted into "totem," probably spread through North America with Indian traders during the 1800s.

Are there different types of totem poles? Yes. The huge carved wooden figures that Europeans first observed were called greet or welcome figures. Often marking the outer limits of a tribe's territory, they were huge single figure totems of a human or an animal. Some held boxes of human remains. Soon after, explorers encountered interior house posts, territory marker poles, house

The traditional hat, eyebrows, eyes, nostrils, lips, and fingers
indicate this is a human figure.

frontal entrance poles, and heraldic or free-standing totems. There were also memorial totem poles and boxes.

Is there such a thing as a "ridicule" pole? Yes, there is a long tradition of ridiculing others on totems. Sometimes a chief might be carved a little too naked, though usually he was too embarrassed to raise the pole. Other times, the crests of thieves or images of bearded white persons were put on display to embarrass the wrongdoer.

What are the primary things to look for, in "seeing" a totem pole? To understand what you're looking at on totem poles, it's useful to recognize four characteristic shapes that you'll see in totem art: the ovoid, U-shape, split-U, and the elongated S-shape. The ovoid is an oval with flattened corners that can be used alone or as nested ovoids stacked one inside the other. An ovoid often indicates a shoulder, elbow, or knee joint that moves; other times it's a basic space-filler. The U-shape is often used for wing feathers and has a rhythmic form often found with the split-U. Rather like a candy kiss, the split-U divides the U-shape in two. The elongated S, used in groups, often depicts an animal's ribs.

Are there extra eyes hidden on totems? Rarely. The ovoid shape used in totem forms is sometimes mistaken for an eye. However, eyes are clearly delineated with a pupil and an eyelid that is pinched at both corners.

Are animal body parts sometimes carved out of order? Yes. In certain cases, though more in two-dimensional work than on totem poles, animal or bird figures are split or fragmented, with eyes, joints, legs, fins, wings, or tails appearing out of place. For example, the blowhole for a whale might appear in the center of its dorsal fin.

Are creatures nested inside other creatures on totem poles? Yes. One creature often appears inside another. For example, Bear Mother's cubs can be hidden in her ears, a man can be curled up inside a Whale, or Frog can pop out of a figure's mouth.

Are materials other than wood used in totem poles? Occasionally other materials such as horn, copper, hair, teeth, mirrors, or opercula shells are inlaid for decoration, but these tend to disappear quickly. A new totem in the state of Washington, carved by properly sanctioned Alaska master carvers, has blown-glass accessories and neon tubing incorporated into it.

Are there different ways to finish a totem? While most totems are sanded smooth, a few are sandblasted to raise the grain, and a very few are

Finishing techniques include feathering (above left), an intricate finish, or smoothing with incised marks (above right). Below, four characteristic shapes include the U-shape (left), the elongated-S (right), the split-U (bottom left), and nested ovoids (bottom right).

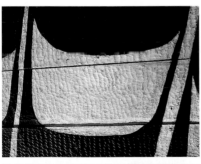
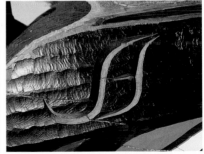

"feathered," an exacting technique produced by creating rows of adz marks along the surface that offer an interesting texture.

Do other aboriginal people make totem poles? Yes. The Ainu people, living on Hokkaido Island in northern Japan, create pole groupings. Some are topped with an animal such as Bear that is sacred to them. And in New Zealand, the Maori people carve house posts said to represent dead ancestors. The first Hawaiians produced totem-like figures called *tikis*. These too represented ancestors and were associated with taboos. No artistic link has been established among these Pacific Rim peoples, though the possibilities are intriguing.

Totem Bight's collection includes this Tlingit Octopus, once known as Devilfish, with tentacles and sucker cups.

What are some distinctive features of Alaska totems? Compared with the southern tribes who practice the totem tradition, story figures such as Raven Liberating the Sun, Duk-toothl, Gonakadet (Sea Wolf), and Devilfish (Octopus) are portrayed frequently and expressively in Alaska. Alaska Natives carve more human beings, especially beautiful women in regalia. In Alaska, master carvers occasionally portray themselves or their tools on their totems, and Tlingit totem poles display a rich green blue color unique to the region.

Who are some of today's Alaska carvers? Some of Alaska's carvers include David A. Boxley and his son David R. Boxley, Will Burkhart, Bruce Cook, Frank L. Fulmer, John Hagen, Wayne Hewson, Greg Horner, Joe Jacobs, Nathan Jackson and his son Stephen Jackson, Norman G. Jackson, Duane Pasco, Wayne Price, Israel Shotridge, Ernest Smeltzer, David Svenson, and Lee Wallace.

How old is the totem tradition? It's impossible to know when the Natives of the North Pacific Coast first began to carve and paint crests on their possessions, but the tradition may have evolved over thousands of years. At one archaeological site in British Columbia, diggers carbon-dated a 600-year-old bone comb carved with a recognizable Wolf crest. Alaska's petroglyphs may be older, but stone is impossible to carbon-date.

Do we know the origin of totem poles? No. Before the widespread use of metal tools, Pacific Northwest totem poles were probably fewer and smaller. A traditional item known as a "talking stick" displayed a person's crests. Some speculate that talking sticks evolved into totem poles.

From what type of wood are totems made? The preferred material is Western red cedar, *Thuja plicata*, a wood that carves easily yet holds its edge for many years. Some totems are made from Alaska yellow cedar, *Chamaecyparis nootkatensis*, a similar type of wood.

How old is an average totem pole? Unless totems have been treated with resistant chemicals or have been sheltered indoors, after 60 to 100 years most totems begin to decompose. They eventually fall over, decay, and return to the earth.

Ancient petroglyphs on the beach near Wrangell are probably thousands of years old.

Where are the oldest totem poles located? The oldest and largest collection of totem fragments is housed in the Totem Heritage Center in Ketchikan, Alaska. The 33 fragments in this collection, considered invaluable for research purposes, are about 100 years old. The oldest collection of totem poles *in situ* are at a World Heritage Site called Ninstints on the Queen Charlotte Islands (Haida Gwaii) of British Columbia, Canada, just southwest of the Alaska Panhandle. They probably date from about the 1850s.

Where is the oldest totem art in Alaska? Petroglyph Beach, a state historic park in Wrangell, has the highest concentration of petroglyphs in Southeast Alaska. Petroglyphs are ancient designs or symbols pecked into rocks. Some scholars believe that the figures may be thousands of years old. Identifiable Northwest Coast Indian ovoid, U-shape, and elongated S-shapes are clearly defined. Additional petroglyphs have been discovered on Kodiak Island, at Cape Alitak, in Glacier Bay, at Ground Hog Bay, near Hydaburg Creek on the west coast of Prince of Wales Island, at Hetta Inlet near Sitka, elsewhere on Baranof Island, on Etolin Island, at Anan Creek near Wrangell, at Wrangell, and near Juneau, including Fritz Cove Road, and elsewhere on Douglas Island. The Alaska Historical Preservation Act of 1971 protects all petroglyphs from destruction, defacing, moving, or excavating.

What happens to old totem poles? For the first 50 years of the twentieth century, several methods were pioneered to preserve old totems. Some tried creosote, glues, and adhesives, or rock salt, while others replicated totems in fiberglass. No method to replace decayed wood was ever completely satisfactory. Traditionally, old totems were allowed to lie where they fell until a relative of the original family that owned the totem could afford to have it replicated. The replica was raised with great ceremony and had the same status as the one it replaced. Occasionally, the totem just decayed and became one with the earth again. From 1850–1950, many were collected as soon as they began to tilt.

What is the connection between kinfolk and totem crests? Ancient Alaskan totem crests originated to define each group's privileges within their traditional tribal kinship systems. Each clan authorized several crests exclusive to them to identify their rights and prerogatives. These crests were then emblazoned on almost everything they owned. Today the Tlingit continue to keep track of their relatives using the old system, the Haida practice a fairly close approximation of their old ways, and the Tsimshian are hosting potlatches to reestablish their old clan affiliations.

What is a "prerogative"? Prerogatives are privileges that nobody else has. Rights, on the other hand, are legitimate titles or privileges, but other folks may share all or part of these advantages with you.

What are examples of totem rights and prerogatives? Totem crests indicated which household had entitlements to the best fishing spots, fur-trading privileges, game hunting areas, berry patches, and trade routes. Other crests signified the order of privilege for wearing masks and ceremonial regalia, owning the best art works, making rules for the household, enjoying privacy screens, telling stories, and being served food. Every facet of life was regulated down to the seat a person occupied in the transport canoe. For example, if a whale were found dead, the daughter of the hunter who found it had the prerogative to touch it first and choose the choicest pieces of meat from it. Next came the rights of the chief and his household, and so on. Even the spirit world was involved: there were rules about who could pray to which spirits for favors.

Where is the world's tallest totem? You decide. The evidence is presented on page 83 of this book.

What is the relationship between potlatches and totem poles? Traditionally, totem poles were raised as part of a complex ceremony called a potlatch. Both the totem and the potlatch solidified a Native person's kinship, rights, and status. Today, a person can commission a totem pole and it is permissible to raise it during its own ceremony, not necessarily as part of a potlatch.

INTERPRETING TOTEM FIGURES

TOTEM ACCESSORY OR POSE	MEANING
Blank space on most of the totem, scored or unscored	Called skils, this is known as the "prestige of open space"
Box or rectangular shape on top	Memorial to a deceased elder
Cane or stick in hand	Talking stick; a policy-maker who gives speeches
Chilkat blanket or design	Wealth, prestige, honor, high rank
Curled up tightly in submission	A slave
Figure head-down	Clan defeated at one time, lost rights to this crest, but displays it anyway
Figure in a horizontal position or figure head-up	Crest earned in victorious battle
Figures inside ears	Humor; or offspring
Hand out, palm up	Welcome; or a wish to share knowledge
Hand up like a stop sign	Stay away, you are in someone's territory
Hat with rings	Each ring beyond the first represents a potlatch celebration the person has hosted; four rings means three potlatches.
Holding hands	A modern pole; cooperation or unity
Labret or lip plug	Prestigious or honorable person ➤

Is it true that there are totem poles spread all over the world? Yes. Because North America's Natives were seen as a "dying people" in the early 1900s, collectors from all over the world scoured the Pacific Northwest and Alaska for masks, regalia, and totem poles. It is possible to see authentic old totems in museums in Australia, Canada, Finland, France, Germany, and many other countries as well as throughout the United States. And in the past half century, commissions for contemporary totems have come from many nations.

Are authentic totem poles still carved? There are excellent carvers alive today who understand the tradition and carve remarkable, skilled, authentic totems.

How has the totem tradition changed over the years? Like all great art traditions, totem styles have altered and merged. A carver may borrow aesthet-

INTERPRETING TOTEM FIGURES continued

TOTEM ACCESSORY OR POSE	MEANING
Materials other than cedar	Copper is a sign of prestige; glass or mirrors were once the prerogative of warriors who threw crystal "bombs"
Naked, unclothed portions, front or back	Hidden protest, usually about too much non-Native interference
On its haunches, animal with human feet, or a human with animal parts	A spirit figure with the ability to transform from one form to another
Round, thick necklace	Cedar rope necklace indicating shaman
Shield-shaped object or extra face	A potlatch copper or implied copper face on the chest shows that this is the carver's first official pole; or the totem's owner is high ranking
Shrimp or small crab in a figure's mouth	Symbol of thievery
Smaller figure in larger figure's arms	Offspring, or founder of a new family line
Three or four little men with hats on top	Watchmen mean protection
Tongue thrusting	Passing on knowledge or power; if thrust at the viewer, the knowledge is for them
Upside-down face	In the old days, a protest that the carvers were not treated properly; today done for comic relief.
Woman's crown or lip plug	Prestigious or honorable woman

ically pleasing figures or details from another tribe's totems. Ever-greater proficiency has eliminated those artists with marginal talent. Some of today's artists are traditionalists, whereas others enjoy stylistic innovation. Even carvers with the highest standards acknowledge that some of the best work they've seen was done by their ancestors.

Are any of the poles in Alaska's totem parks fake? No, they are not fakes. Many totem park poles are replicas of earlier totems that stood in other locations but have decayed. Replicating totems is a valid part of the tradition. Old Native carved wooden items, from dugout canoes to cedar bowls, have been replicated for centuries. The important consideration is that the crests and forms are rendered as faithfully as possible.

How can a person get an authentic totem carved for him/her? In Haines, Sitka, and Ketchikan, there are centers where master carvers will consider creating authentic totems for anyone with $10,000 as a down payment. Prices go up from there. Famous carvers have Web sites. Also see www.alaskanativeartists.com.

How long does it take to carve a totem? A totem pole can be carved in about 3 weeks to 3 months, depending on the size of the final pole.

What is the protocol for raising old totems far from Alaska? It is proper to research as much factual information about the totem as possible. A Native person who truly understands the totem tradition should be sought out. Flakes of old paint should be color matched. It is not proper to change the original colors or to paint parts that were originally unpainted. Elders from a local Indian tribe should be consulted even if they are not from the totem tradition. If you live in their traditional territory, it is proper to follow their protocol for the raising ceremony—including meals and gifts. During the ceremony, someone should speak of the totem's history and tell the stories of the crests.

Is the "low man on the totem pole" the least important? No. The low man has the same importance as other figures. Because viewers see the carver's ability close-up, the lowest figure is sometimes the only figure a famous-name carver has personally produced—in a sense making it even more important.

Do the "accessories" or poses on totem poles mean anything? The accessories or poses on totems once aided the viewer in interpreting the details of a pole. Examples are provided in the sidebar.

OLD CRESTS, MODERN MEANINGS

TOTEM FIGURE	DERIVED MEANING TODAY	EXAMPLE(S)
Bear	Concerned parent, founder, kind person with family values, a noble death	Parent
Beaver	Good marksman, systematically undermines enemies, skilled, wants peace but will fight	Tradesperson, gun collector, soldier
Blackfish (Killer Whale)	Strength, others are jealous, victory after defeat	Sports hero
Dogfish Woman	Noble air, social climber, friend of Frogs	Charity matron
Eagle, Thunderbird	Admired, an inspired presence, magnificent	Pilot, star
Fog Woman	Clever, competent, fruitful, a beauty, changes climate for the better	Wife, weather announcer
Frog	Self-made, wealth obtained through own efforts, goes through fire and emerges alive	Entrepreneur, skilled artisan
Hawk	Keen hunter, searcher, vanquishes vermin	Law enforcement officer
Land Otter Person	Overcomes depression; descends into crawling state then rises up again	Therapist, counselor
Mosquito	Taste for blood, turns to ash, bad reputation overcome	Reformed criminal
Octopus (Devilfish)	Overcomes vice, refuses to be drowned	Reformed addict
Owl	Messenger, changes coldness to warmth, links with the spirit world, comforts the bereaved	Clergy person, funeral arranger, nurse
Raven	Intelligent, talkative, noble (but secretly seen as greedy), powerful enough to change society, hides misdeeds	Politician, bureaucrat, lawyer
Salmon	Sacrifices to give others a chance, respects the environment, understands cycles	Environmentalist, teacher
Sea Wolf	Fearsome, stealthy hunter, cunning, secretive, fights exhaustion, rejoices in a watery world, brings luck to others	Submarine crewmember, detective
Sooty Skin	Overcomes ridicule, trains diligently, meets the test, scares others, forgives enemies	Immigrant, athlete
Wolf	Listens to the beat, heals others, goes out at night, knows the spirit world	Physician, performer

How are old crests interpreted on totems today? Because outsiders can not claim to have the rights to a Native family crest within the old Alaskan kinship system, today's carvers reinterpret old stories searching for links with the new owner's experiences. They sometimes use ancient crest figures within these interpretations. See the sidebar.

Is there ever humor in a totem pole? Alaska's totem makers occasionally entertain viewers with carved figures peering from ears or upside-down faces. Humor in totem poles, rendered more frequently among Canadian tribes of the Totem People, includes smiley faces, trapdoors in entrance totems, and holes from which to spray water on passersby.

Do totem poles have secrets associated with them? Yes. The carver usually, but not always, carves secret details into the pole and shares the secrets with the pole's owners.

Is it true that a slave used to be buried at the base of old totems? No. While this was once claimed to be fact, when hundreds of old totems were dug up in the 1930s and 1940s, no bones were ever found.

Has political correctness shaped the totem tradition? Yes. Some of the old cannibal figures are no longer carved, bare-breasted female figures are becoming a no-no, and colorful creatures, even Raven, deemed too frightening, too flawed, or too obnoxious, are being reformed.

Are souvenir totems considered real? Native artists began to carve small model poles for sale as souvenirs to tourists more than 100 years ago. If the carver of the totem is skilled and has based the design on the principles of the tradition, it is an authentic totem.

Where can a person learn to carve totem poles? A few non-Native people have merited the privilege of becoming an apprentice to an experienced totem carver. Places of learning include Alaska Arts, Inc., in Haines, the Alaska Heritage Center in Anchorage, the Totem Heritage Center in Ketchikan, and the Southeast Alaska Cultural Center in Sitka.

Where can a person get tools to carve totems? Most carvers make their own tools, but beginners can contact Preferred Edge, www.preferrededge.ca. This company has supplied master carvers including Calvin Hunt, Mervin Child, and Nathan P. Jackson.

May I ask the author questions about totem poles? Yes. Go to www.totemsnet.com. ∎

CHAPTER

Visiting Alaska's Totem Poles

Anchorage

Though geographically beyond the range of the Totem People, Anchorage's historic facilities strive to represent a cross-section of Alaska's Native cultures. Though there are few actual totem poles in Anchorage, a fine collection of Native art is permanently exhibited at the International Airport and in the downtown area. The few totems that are on public display include two small Tlingit totems at the Alaska Railroad station (411 West First Avenue) and two more at the Alaska State Courthouse (825 West Fourth Avenue). Carved by Lee Wallace and Edwin DeWitt, the latter two are called *Attaining a Balance Within*. One depicts how Raven stole the sun and the other shows Eagle Boy stealing Giant Clam. New totems were installed in Fall 2004 at the Alaska Native Medical Center (4315 Diplomacy Drive, 907-563-2662). Native artists also sell their craft goods in the lobby.

The Anchorage Museum of History and Art (121 West Seventh Avenue, open daily, May 15–September 15, then Tuesday–Sunday, admission fee,

Woman Holding a Land Otter **pole in Juneau is the creation of Haida carver John Wallace.**

Tlingit dancer in Chilkat blanket (left). Tlingit creation myth totem pole with Eagle (right), next to Governor's Mansion, Juneau.

907-343-4326) features educational programs including classes, tours, lectures, performances, and films. In addition, the museum houses a permanent collection of Native artifacts numbering some 19,500 objects and more than 350,000 historical photographs including many of totem poles. Seven galleries devoted to the "Art of the North" display early paintings of Alaska.

Surrounded by the majestic Chugach Mountains, the Alaska Native Heritage Center (8800 Heritage Center Drive, daily, June–September, then by arrangement, admission fee, 907-330-8000) presents an interpretive experience of Alaska's primary indigenous groups including workshops, demonstrations, and guided tours of indoor exhibits and outdoor village sites.

Angoon

The Tlingit village of Angoon (community association, 907-788-3411), the main settlement on Admiralty Island, is one of the warmest, driest communities in the Southeast. The community, 60 air miles south of Juneau, is served by air and ferry service. The town's culture and traditions are reflected in nine totem poles by Wayne Price with Donald Frank as his apprentice, and Ray Peck. Most of the 700-plus residents depend on commercial fishing, subsistence hunting, and food gathering. Mysteriously disappearing from Angoon in 1908, a red cedar totem pole dubbed *Totem Teddy* was repatriated in 2003 by members of the *Teikweidi*, or Bear Clan.

Fairbanks

Although the Interior is well outside the traditional homelands of the Totem People, two poles by Amos Wallace are on display in the Alaskaland Pioneer Park, located on Airport Way. Admission is free to the park, which features special theme areas such as a mining valley, a Gold Rush town, and a Native village. Call 907-459-1095 for more information.

Hoonah

Glacial advances from A.D. 1400 to about 1750 drove the Glacier Bay Huna people from their homes, across Icy Strait, to Hoonah, "village by the cliff," located on an ice-free natural harbor on Chichagof Island, 40 air miles west of Juneau. Marketing the destination as "Port Icy Strait," select cruise lines stop at this tiny Tlingit village (907-789-1773). Cruise ship visitors come ashore to see a restored cannery, a few retail outlets, a totem carving hut, and a Native cultural center including a Tlingit dance troupe. The Native village itself, about 2 miles away, is accessible via floatplane or the Alaska ferry system. The ferry stops for an hour so passengers can view four notable totems.

Juneau

The mountain-bound capital city of Alaska is the headquarters for several of the state's most important Native organizations. During the first week of June in even-numbered years, the city of Juneau and the Sealaska Heritage Institute (907-463-4844) host Celebration, featuring thousands of Tlingit, Haida, and Tsimshian people in ceremonial regalia. For everyday visitors, the Juneau Douglas City Museum (Fourth and Main Streets, 907-586-3572) provides a map for a self-guided walking tour of Juneau's national register of totem poles. Walkers start with the *Harnessing the Atom* and *Four Story Totems* located outside the City Museum (Calhoun and Main Streets). Next comes the *Friendship Totem Pole* (Courthouse lobby, Fourth and Seward), *The Waasgo* or *Old Witch Totem*

(Main floor lobby, State Office Building), the *Governor's Totem Pole*, a creation story with its Mosquito figure (716 Calhoun Street), *Raven and Eagle Totems* (Village Street and Willoughby), and the *Wooshkeetaan, and Aak'w Tribe Totem Poles* (101 Egan Drive). Also within easy walking distance is a Native creation myth mural featuring Raven, found on the City Municipal Building (Marine Park facing Marine Way).

Two Native-owned galleries include the Raven–Eagle Gift Shop (Goldbelt Mount Roberts Tramway) and the Mount Juneau Trading Post (151 Franklin Street). The four-story white building on the corner of Main and Marine Way is the home of the Sealaska Heritage Institute. Visitors are welcome to come inside and view

This Tlingit totem in Wrangell depicts a copper-eyed Bear Mother protecting her humanlike cub with shell teeth and hair.

two poles in the lobby by Warren Peale and Nathan Jackson, plus a canoe, wall screens, and exquisite Chilkat robes. On the fourth floor, more exceptional carvings by Jimmy Marks, Ray Peck, and Nathan Jackson are on display, as well as a 100-year-old Haida button blanket.

A replica of a traditional Tlingit plank house with an elaborate painted screen and *Raven and Frog House Posts* can be found at the Alaska State Museum (395 Whittier Street, daily, May 15–September 15, then Tuesday–Saturday, admission fee, 907-465-2901). This worthwhile museum protects an invaluable ceremonial Frog clan potlatch hat, a Chilkat robe woven in the famous Raven's Tail pattern, and the top of the original *President Lincoln Totem*.

A ride on the Goldbelt Mount Roberts Tramway (490 South Franklin Street, admission fee, 907-463-3412) provides an unparalleled view, weather permitting. The trip includes a stop at the Chilkat Theater, where guests see an 18-minute film, view totem-style carvings along the trails, and eat at the

Chinook Restaurant. The House of Wickersham (213 Seventh Street, daily except Wednesday, May 15–October 1, then by appointment, admission fee, 907-586-9001) listed on the National Register of Historic Places, displays an important collection of Native baskets and photographs of early Native culture.

In 1870, the largest permanent Tlingit settlements in the region were the Auk'kw Villages. Long since abandoned, only the Auk Village Recreation Site (Glacier Highway, 18 miles north, 907-586-8800) remains. Before outsiders settled here, clans operated independently within individual territories. Even though all Tlingit people shared language, similar beliefs, and customs, their clans were never united under a rule of one leader or a single governing body.

Kake

Situated between Juneau and Wrangell, Kake (pronounced CAKE) is home to the world's tallest properly sanctioned totem (village office, 907-785-6471). In 1990, three new Tlingit totems were raised here at the uppermost tip of Kupreanof Island. And in 1994, for the first potlatch held in Kake in over a century, *Killer Whale Totem* by Norman and Mike Jackson was raised. Two other

WHERE IS THE WORLD'S TALLEST TOTEM?

Carved from a single tree and placed on a high bluff, the 132-foot Kake, Alaska, totem pole claims to be the world's tallest, properly dedicated, authentic crest-displaying, single-log totem in the world. It probably is. Built to serve as the Alaska Pavilion centerpiece for Japan's 1970 World's Fair, it was dedicated to all tribes in Southeast Alaska.

Two other taller contenders have lesser credentials. The first is the properly sanctioned 173-foot-high Kwakiutl totem in Alert Bay, B.C., Canada, carved from two or three separate cedar pieces telescoped together. Some say its piecemeal construction disqualifies it. The second is the 149-foot-tall single piece totem in Kalama, Washington. The Kalama pole was created by a non-Native who adopted the name "Lelooska." The *Guinness Book of World Records* documents it as the world's tallest totem pole.

And two totems, the world's tallest in their day, are reluctant to give up their claims to being the world's tallest. One, raised in 1956, is Mungo Martin's 127-foot, 7-inch totem in Victoria, B.C.'s, Beacon Hill Park, and the second from the year 1903, now in Tacoma, Washington, at Fireman's Park measures in at a mere 105 feet. ●

new totems, *Raven and Eagle*, overlook Little Gunnuk Creek. Occasionally the Keex' Kwaan Tlingit Dancers perform in traditional regalia.

Ketchikan

For visitors with time for only one totem-viewing stop, Ketchikan is the place to visit. Nearly 70 totem poles stand in this city that occupies former Tlingit territory. Derived from the Kichxaan dialect and meaning "thundering eagle wings," Ketchikan raised the first *Kadjuk Totem* or *Chief Johnson Pole* (Totem Way and Stedman Street) back in 1905. Today, an eagle sculpture, *Thundering Wings*, by Tlingit master carver Nathan Jackson, is perched near the dock, and the *Chief Kyan Totem Pole* (Mission Street) towers over tiny Whale Park.

The Westmark Cape Fox Lodge (800 Venetia Way, 907-225-8001), accessible by funicular tram, is fronted by the *Council of the Clans*—six 12-foot totems by master carver Lee Wallace. Common areas within the hotel display carved masks and painted house screens as well as silkscreen prints.

The Discovery Center (50 Main Street, daily, May–September, then Tuesday–Saturday, admission fee, 907-228-6214) is just steps from the cruise ship dock. Operated by the USDA Forest Service, the center's foyer displays three totems carved in the Haida, Tlingit, and Tsimshian styles carved by Jim Hart (Chief Edenshaw), Israel Shotridge, and David A. Boxley, respectively. Inside the Native Traditions Room, visitors can explore a Native fish camp and see traditional wooden implements.

Authentic Pacific Northwest Coast Indian art is easy to find along bustling Creek Street. Fog Woman, the female figure on the *Creek Street Totem*, attracts not only salmon but thousands of two-legged visitors as well. Two Native-owned galleries are Hide-A-Way Gifts (18 Creek Street, 907-225-8626) and Alaska Eagle Arts (5 Creek Street, Ste. 3, 907-225-8365). Outside the Tongass Historical Museum (629 Dock Street, daily, May 15–September 30, then afternoons, Wednesday–Sunday, admission fee, 907-225-5600) stands *Raven Stealing the Sun* carved by Tlingit Dempsey Bob. Inside is a small exhibit of Tlingit, Haida, and Tsimshian artifacts.

Listed on the National Register of Historic Places, the Totem Heritage Center (601 Deermont Street, daily, May 15–September 30, then Tuesday–Friday afternoons, admission fee, 907-225-5900) is the storage place for 33 unrestored nineteenth-century totem poles and wood fragments. About

Two Raven totem guards flank a Tlingit clan house, where visitors come to watch Native dancing demonstrations at Saxman Totem Park, Ketchikan.

100 years old, they were removed from deserted Tlingit and Haida villages throughout Southeast Alaska. Considered the largest, oldest collection of authentic totems in the world, the center was established in 1976 to display this irreplaceable collection. Carvers and researchers consider them an important resource. The center also promotes the traditional arts and crafts of the Tlingit, Haida, and Tsimshian people. Nearby there is a self-guided nature trail located beside Ketchikan Creek, across from the Tribal Hatchery, and live Eagle Center.

Fourteen totems and a to-scale Raven Tribal House replica stand along a trail in the forest at Totem Bight State Park (Milepost 10 North, Tongass Highway, daily, year-round, dawn to dusk, donation, 907-247-8574). This collection was created in 1938 by Native artists in the CCC. Carved interior house posts symbolize Duk-toothl, a hero wearing a weaselskin hat. The stylized Raven painting on the house and the *Wandering Raven House Entrance Pole* by 1940s-era carver Charles Brown indicate that the occupants were upper class. On each exterior corner post sits a tattooed potlatch man with a spruce root hat and a "talking stick." Architect Linn Forrest supervised construction of this model Native village, first called Mud Bight. Workers laid fragments of old poles beside freshly cut cedar logs, and then replicated them. Tools were handmade, modeled on older tools used before the coming of the explorers. Artisans created a natural pallet of colors using clamshells, lichen, graphite, copper, pebbles, and salmon eggs. Nature's colors were then simulated with modern paints. At statehood in 1959, title to this important site passed from the federal government to the State of Alaska, and the site was added to the National Register of Historic Places in 1970.

Popular Saxman Totem Park and Native Village (Milepost 2.5 South, daily, year-round, admission fee, 907-225-4846) is the leading totem collection in Southeast Alaska. Visitors walk along a spectacular avenue of totem poles up the hill to a gift shop to purchase tickets. Next comes the carving shed, where carvers are often present, and the Beaver clan house, where dancers put on periodic demonstrations. Encompassing some 30 totem poles replicated from an old Cape Fox village at Kirk Point, Tongass, Village, and Pennock Islands, each of the totems has a distinctive story to tell. Of special note are the *President Lincoln Totem* and a totem depicting a crouching man with a Giant Rock Oyster holding him fast. The Cape Fox Dancers perform here periodically, and carvers are often present to answer questions. Here, master carver Nathan P. Jackson and his apprentice Tim Long produce prestigious totem poles.

Klukwan and Haines

Over 300 years ago, certain Tlingit clans from Prince of Wales Island, the Stikine River valley, the Nass River valley, and Kupreanof Island migrated north and established villages at Klukwan—the Mother Village—and at six other sites. The people of this area came to be known as the Chilkat and the Chilkoot peoples. They carried on an active trade over closely guarded mountain passes with Interior tribes. To keep their routes secret from foreign traders, the Natives would meet ships at the end of the Chilkat Peninsula, far from the grease trails over which they transported guns, iron, tools, blankets, regalia, and eulachon butter. Skilled at traveling in large, oceangoing canoes, the northern Tlingit also traded by sea with more southerly Tlingit people, who in turn traveled as far south as Puget Sound, Washington, and perhaps northern California.

About 22 miles north of Haines, the traditional Tlingit community of Klukwan, located on the north bank of the Chilkat River, is the only remaining village. Considered the citadel of Tlingit art, it is known for its Chilkat blankets

A Tsimshian family, members of the Eagle clan, pose in their dance regalia.

---

and dance robes woven from mountain goat hair and cedar bark. The village is currently developing a Cultural Heritage Center and Museum.

In 1881, Chilkat Indians from the now-abandoned village of Yandestaki, negotiating with Presbyterian minister Dr. Sheldon Jackson, ceremonially received Jackson's friend, S. Hall Young, who was to build a mission and school. The site chosen was known as Dei shu, "the end of the trail." There were as yet no buildings on the site that was later to become the town of Haines. Rev. Eugene Willard and his wife, Caroline, soon arrived to carry on the missionary work. The mission was renamed Haines in 1884 in honor of Mrs. F. E. Haines, who chaired the National Committee that had raised funds for the mission's construction. Canneries started up in the area, prospectors traveled through on their way to the ancient trade routes over the Chilkoot and White Passes, and with the advent of the Gold Rush, many newcomers arrived. The town of Haines grew up around the mission site, and Fort Seward was built nearby.

Today Chilkat blankets and Tlingit slatted wooden armor as well as Russian trade goods are on display at the Sheldon Museum and Cultural Center (Main and First Street, daily, May 15–September 15, then limited hours, admission fee, 907-766-2366).

Fort William H. Seward welcomes visitors to view Alaskan artists and carvers periodically working their trades including totem carving, silkscreen making, and silver carving. Workshops are also available for those who would like to learn totem pole carving alongside master carvers (Alaska Indian Arts, Hospital Building 13, Fort Seward, Monday to Friday, tuition fee, 907-766-2160). The facility includes officers' headquarters, barracks, a tribal house, a trapper's cabin, and a cache (a structure on stilts to protect food from the bears and other critters).

Starting from the town of Haines, a company named Keet Gooshi Tours offers a 3-hour cultural tour to the Tlingit village of Klukwan (June–September, two trips daily, fee, 907-766-2168). The tour

Rainbow Man tops this Tsimshian totem in Metlakatla. He stands on a human holding a "copper," a symbol of wealth and authority.

covers the Chilkat Bald Eagle Reserve, the Chilkat River, Native tribal house interiors, Eagle and Raven clan wall screens, and totem poles. Participants also taste Native fry bread and learn how the Tlingit once rendered eulachon fish into "Indian butter."

Metlakatla

Today, about 1,200 Tsimshian people live in Metlakatla, Alaska's only Indian reservation, 15 oceangoing miles south of Ketchikan. Several old Tlingit totems were standing on the beach when 823 Tsimshian from Canada arrived on August 7, 1887. Missionary William Duncan had negotiated with President Grover Cleveland to secure the entire expanse of Annette Island for them to settle. Enforcing strict rules against alcohol and cleaning up the village to his exacting Victorian standards, Duncan respected Tsimshian traditions but felt that totem carving was a waste of time. Against the backdrop of this philosophy, most of the original totems were destroyed, though two were shipped to Sheldon Jackson's museum in Sitka.

Starting in the 1970s, several villagers dedicated themselves to becoming culture bearers and relearning their forgotten traditions. A dance troupe was formed and young men began carving as apprentices. After much study, carver David A. Boxley raised the first Metlakatla totem in 1982. During the next 15 years, he and his son David R. Boxley, along with noted carver Wayne Hewson, created more than 42 poles and numerous art pieces. Among them, they carved 11 of the 13 totems now standing in Metlakatla. Private or group guided tours of Metlakatla village, including the Rev. Duncan's Cottage and the town totem poles, are available through Pat Beal, Tourism Director, 907-886-8687. In summer, the residents staff a small craft market that is open when visitors are in town.

Prince of Wales Island

Of the approximately 1,800 Haida people now residing in Alaska, about 300 live on Prince of Wales Island. During the late 1600s, a group of Haida migrated to this enormous island from British Columbia's Queen Charlotte Islands. Here they discovered abundant resources and several abandoned Tlingit villages, where they built their own clan houses and added their own totem poles.

Today their descendants live in Craig and Klawock, about 7 miles apart, and in Hydaburg, 30 miles from Craig. In Craig there is a small Haida

Sailors of the late 1800s introduced Haida carvers to scrimshaw crosshatching.

totem park on the waterfront, and Klawock has a totem park with about 21 totem poles listed on the National Register of Historic Places. The most notable is *Girl with a Woodworm Totem.* Some totems here are original and some were replicated from the previously occupied village of Tuxekan, an abandoned Tlingit village on the northern half of Prince of Wales Island.

Seattle, Washington

Seattle is also a good place to view Alaska totems. With its long history as a staging stop on the way to and from Alaska, Seattle's collectors, tourists, missionaries, gold miners, traders, and trappers were some of the first outsiders to acquire and sell Alaskan Native arts and crafts more than a century ago. Alaska's fishing fleet still berths in Seattle, and the city continues to supply various Alaskan needs and vice versa.

Twin totems carved by Quinault sculptor Marvin Oliver and James Bender stand near the Pike Place Market at Victor Steinbrueck Park. The most famous totem landmark in Seattle is nearby: the *Goodwill Pole* in Pioneer Square.

The Tlingit Goodwill Pole in Seattle's Pioneer Square has a storied history.

A complex totem, Alaska's major emblems are represented: Raven, Bear, Eagle, Killer Whale, and Wolf. Several downtown Seattle galleries specialize in Northwest Coast Native art representing notable Pacific Northwest and Southeast Alaska Native artists.

The Burke Museum (University of Washington, 17 Avenue NE and NE 45 Street, daily except holidays, admission and parking fees, 206-543-5590) usually features a famous Alaskan master carver in attendance several days a week working on a totem pole or major wooden item such as a mask. Near the entrance are two replica totems by master carver Bill Holm. These include a replicated Haida house front pole, first carved in the 1870s, and a Tsimshian memorial pole from the 1880s. Standing nearby, a totemic Killer Whale sculpture, *Single Fin*, from the abandoned village of Howkan, on Prince of Wales Island, was replicated from a nineteenth-century grave marker.

At the turn of the twentieth century, collector John H. Hauberg brought back many articles from Alaska's Tlingit and Haida cultures, now on display at the Seattle Art Museum (100 University Street, Tuesday–Saturday, admission fee, 206-654-3100). In 1991, the museum acquired the John H. Hauberg Collection, including almost 200 Native American masks, sculpture, textiles, and decorative and household objects from the Pacific Northwest, British Columbia, and Alaska.

There are some brightly painted totem poles at the Daybreak Star Indian Cultural Center (Discovery Park, West Government Way at 36th Avenue, daily, closes at dusk, free, 206-285-4425). And the Tillicum Village Tour (Piers 55 and 56, fee, 206-443-1244) takes visitors on a boat ride to nearby Blake Island where a barbecue salmon dinner is served in a model clan house while Northwest Native dancers put on a performance.

Sitka

Built on the site of an ancient Tlingit village, in the shelter of Baranof Island and the shadow of volcanic Mount Edgecumbe, Sitka is located in a particularly striking setting. Its Tlingit names were *Sheet Ka* and *Shee Atika* meaning "the village behind the islands." Sitka's unique Tlingit, Aleut, and Russian heritage combine in delightful ways throughout this university town.

SEATTLE'S GOODWILL TOTEM

Goodwill has many shades of meaning, but rarely rises to such ironic levels. In 1899, a goodwill mission traveled to Alaska to celebrate Seattle's lucrative links with that gold-producing region. While cruising home on the steamship *City of Seattle*, and reportedly well fortified with intoxicants, the delegates spotted a fine Tlingit totem pole near Port Tongass, Alaska. Thinking the seaside village abandoned, crewmen rowed ashore, cut down the pole, and loaded it aboard before steaming away. Returning to their village, residents were stunned at the pilfering, protested through letters, then sent delegations south to Seattle.

The totem, raised in a well-publicized civic ceremony, stayed put—though in due course, the perpetrators paid a small fine for their transgression. In 1938, an arsonist set the pole aflame, and in 1941, as part of the CCC program, descendants of the villagers were paid to replicate it. As a gesture of goodwill, they officially presented the storied totem to the city. Seattle restored the Tlingit totem pole standing in Pioneer Square once again in 1972, and five years later had it declared a National Landmark. ●

The Sitka Tribe of Alaska Community House (200 Katlian Street, admission fee, 907-747-7290) offers periodic presentations of Native dances, as well as seasonal walking or bus tours of the town. To see ceremonial Chilkat blankets periodically in-the-making, and the works of over 100 Alaska artists, drop into the Sitka Rose Gallery (419 Lincoln Street, open year-round, 907-747-3030).

In the 1890s, the Rev. Dr. Sheldon Jackson, a Presbyterian missionary, acquired nearly 5,000 traditional items including dozens of carvings of argillite, a soft black slate favored by Haida carvers. His collection can be viewed at the Sheldon Jackson Museum (104 College Drive, daily, May 15–September 15, then Tuesday–Saturday, admission fee, 907-747-8981).

Totem seekers must see the combined Sitka National Historical Park (103 Monastery Street, 907-747-0110) and Southeast Alaska Indian Cultural Center (106 Metlakatla Street, daily, in summer, then shorter hours, by donation, 907-747-8061). Located on traditional Kiks.ádi land and first set aside as a park in 1890 by President Benjamin Harrison, the site includes 15 restored poles in a serene section of temperate rain forest with two miles of wooded pathways. Some were copied from a Haida village on Prince of Wales Island; others are from the local Tlingit tradition. The latter include *K'alyaan, Wolf, Frog/Raven, Trader Legend, Raven Memorial, Mosquito Legend,* and *Raven/Shark* poles. John Brady, governor of the Alaska Territory from 1897 to 1906, brought the original collection of totems to this spot. The park's visitor center features exhibits on Tlingit culture, and a slide program on the 1804 Battle of Sitka. A wing of the visitor center houses the Southeast Alaska Indian Cultural Center, an independent organization of Tlingit artists who demonstrate traditional wood and silver carving during various hours in tourist season. In front of the center stands the 35-foot *Haa leelk'u has Kaa sta heeni deiy,* a multiclan pole commemorating the Kaagwaantaan, Kiks.ádi, and Coho clans—the three Tlingit-speaking groups who lived in the area before the Russians arrived.

Wrangell

Situated at the mouth of the Stikine River, Wrangell (pronounced RANG-ul) is home to the Tlingit who arrived here about 1,000 years ago and proceeded to dominate commerce in the area. About 1870, thousands of scruffy miners began to appear on their ancient grease trails, searching for gold. Schools and missions followed, and in the 1930s the Bureau of Indian Affairs brought Native people from all over Alaska here for job training.

The town's major attraction is the restored Chief Shakes Tribal House of the Bear (Front Street, closed except during tour ship visits and by appointment, admission fee, 907-874-2023), which is surrounded by rustling cottonwood trees and a dozen historically important totem poles including *Double Killer Whale Crest Hat* and *Grizzly Bear* mortuary totems. An interpreter periodically provides the history of the house interior, while visitors view the magnificent *Frog House Posts* of the Kiks.ádi clan. The Stikine elders also maintain several Tlingit totems at nearby Kiks'Adi Totem Park. These include the *Killisnoo Beaver, Double Raven,* and *One-Legged Fisherman* pole also known as the *Blind Fisherman.*

A new Wrangell Museum opened in 2004 (Monday–Saturday, May 1– September 30, matching cruise ship port times, admission fee, 296 Outer

THE SHAKES DYNASTY

A piece of Wrangell history, the title "Shakes," also spelled "Shaikes," was originally conferred upon one Tlingit Chief Gushklin. About the year 1700, after a victory against the Nisga'a and Skeena River Tsimshian tribes in British Columbia, Gushklin accepted the tribute of his enemy's defeated chief.

The Shakes dynasty Tlingit clan house was restored by the Civilian Conservation Corps in the 1930s and stands on an island in Wrangell.

Rather than submit to the degradation of being a slave, the prisoner removed his Killer Whale hat, and granted the victor his own name—We-Shakes, later shortened to "Shakes." Shakes I was soon succeeded by his eldest nephew, then his brother. The reign of Ka-shishk, or Shakes III, is remembered for his benevolence. Disguising himself in plain ➤

Drive, 907-874-3770) to safeguard four finely carved Tlingit houseposts originating from about 1740, and thought to be the oldest in existence. The carvings are supplemented by a collection of spruceroot and cedar bark baskets from the turn of the twentieth century, a spruce canoe—one of few in existence—and a collection of Tlingit masks.

Some of the best surviving examples of ancient Native artistic expression are petroglyphs or rock carvings found on boulders along the shore throughout Alaska. Petroglyph Beach near Wrangell has the highest concentration of such petroglyphs in Southeast, and has been designated a State Historic Park. There is a wheelchair accessible boardwalk to a deck overlooking the beach, the Stikine River, and Zimovia Strait. Replicas of several petroglyph designs are displayed on the deck, and visitors who bring some paper and crayons may make rubbings of the etched figures. ■

THE SHAKES DYNASTY continued

clothes, he discovered that his people were tired of the hardships of war. His long reign ended when, aged and blind, he was killed by a falling tree. Many slaves were sacrificed at his funeral. His nephew, Shawt-shugo-ish or Shakes IV, was reputedly the first of the Nan-yan-yi chieftains to see a white man—a trader. A receptacle in the back of a Grizzly Bear totem holds Shawt-shugo-ish's ashes. Kow-ish-te, his nephew, became Shakes V. During his tenure, in 1840, the Russian Fort Dionysius was transferred to Britain's Hudson's Bay Company and renamed Fort Stikine. When the Americans purchased Alaska in 1867, the fort was renamed yet again to Fort Wrangell. Chief Shakes V thus witnessed Russian, British, and finally American occupation—all within his lifetime. A Russian-design wood fence surmounted by two replicated Killer Whales enclose his remains. The Whale originals are displayed in his house. Gush-klin II became Shakes VI, and the Chief Shakes Tribal House, built in 1939 through the auspices of the CCC, was his. Throughout their fortunate lifetimes, through their many potlatches, this dynasty acquired an extraordinary number of traditional goods. These include a dozen totem poles that are often photographed by those visiting his house in Wrangell. Old faded postcards of Shakes's totems, dugout canoe, and clan house are frequently sold through Internet auction sites. ●